101 Ready-to-Use Step-by-Step Commands for Dragon Professional

Michael Shepherd

101 Ready-to-Use Step-by-Step Commands for Dragon Professional

Copyright © 2025 Michael Shepherd. All rights reserved.

First published in 2025 by Michael Shepherd: ASPA MEDIA

Trademarks

Dragon, Dragon Professional Individual, Dragon Professional Group, Dragon NaturallySpeaking, MouseGrid, NaturallySpeaking, DragonPad, DragonBar, and Vocabulary Editor are registered trademarks of Nuance Inc.

Windows 8, Windows 10, Windows 11, MS-DOS, Command Prompt (cmd.exe), MSOffice 2010, Office 365, Microsoft 365, Excel, MS Excel, Excel 2010, Excel 365, Outlook, MS Outlook, Outlook 365, PowerPoint, MS PowerPoint, PowerPoint 2010, PowerPoint 365, Publisher, MS Publisher, Publisher 2010, Publisher 365, Visual Basic, MS Edge, Word, MS Word, Word 2010, and Word 365 are trademarks or registered trademarks of Microsoft Corporation.

MindManager is a registered trademark of Corel Corporation.

Adobe Photoshop is a registered trademark of Adobe Inc. (formerly Adobe Systems Incorporated).

Sublime Text is a registered trademark of Sublime HQ Pty Ltd.

Firefox and Mozilla Thunderbird are registered trademarks of Mozilla Foundation.

Google Chrome, Google Docs, and Google Sheets are registered trademarks of Google LLC.

All terms mentioned in this book that are known to be trademarks or service marks have been appropriately capitalized. Neither the authors nor the publisher (or any of their employees, agents, subcontractors, or assigns) can attest to the accuracy of this information. Use of a term in this book should not be regarded as affecting the validity of any trademark or service mark.

Many of the designations used by manufacturers and sellers to distinguish their products are claimed as trademarks. Where those designations appear in this book, and the authors or the publisher was aware of a trademark claim, the designations appear as requested by the owner of the trademark.

All other product names and services identified throughout this book are used in editorial fashion only and for the benefit of such companies with no intention of infringement of the trademark. No such use, or the use of any trade name, is intended to convey endorsement or other affiliation with this book.

Warning and Disclaimer

The author and publisher have made every effort to make this book as complete and as accurate as possible, but no warranty or fitness is implied. The information provided is on an "as is" basis. The information contained in this book is sold without warranty, either express or implied.

The author and the publisher disclaim all responsibility for errors or omissions, including without limitation responsibility for damages resulting from the use of or reliance on this work.

Neither the authors nor the publisher (or any of their employees, agents, subcontractors, distributors or assigns) has any responsibility for any loss of any kind, including lost profits, arising from your use of any of these code examples.

Use of the information and instructions contained in this book is at your own risk. If any code samples or other technology this work contains or describes is subject to open-source licenses or the intellectual property rights of others, it is your responsibility to ensure that your use thereof complies with such licenses and/or rights.

The example commands (macros) contained in this book are designed to illustrate the potential of how Dragon Professional and Dragon NaturallySpeaking can interact with various applications. Each command will only work with the stated application and are not designed to work impeccably under all conditions; therefore, you should treat them with caution if you decide to use them on anything other than the stated application.

Although every effort has been made to test the commands for errors and eliminate them, errors may unknowingly occur. I strongly suggest that you trial the commands using test documents and re-test, especially if there has been an update to any of the applications.

About the Author

Michael Shepherd is a Dragon-accredited trainer and freelance assistive technology (AT) tutor with more than 35 years of IT experience, including roles as a systems analyst, software developer, and business consultant. He has created and delivered training courses for educational establishments across the UK and internationally.

For the past 15 years, Michael has been teaching university students and workplace professionals how to effectively utilise assistive technology software to support their work. It is his passion for the Dragon software and its benefits, not only for his students but also for businesses and organisations seeking to boost productivity, that has inspired him to share his expertise on the product.

In his spare time, Michael runs a Dragon tutorial site (www.dragonspeechtips.com) where he shares tips and offers support to Dragon users. He also manages a Dragon Professional online resource (www.dragonspeechacademy.com) which features a wealth of online Dragon tutorials. Additionally, Michael creates add-ons for the Dragon Professional software, further enhancing its functionality for users.

Acknowledgments

I would like to extend my sincere thanks to the team at Nuance for their relentless efforts in enhancing the Dragon software application. To my workplace clients, who eagerly embrace the benefits of Dragon software to boost their productivity, your questions and feedback have been instrumental in the creation of this book for all Dragon users.

My gratitude also goes to my students, whose resilience and determination in the face of adversity inspire me daily. To my family and friends, your unwavering encouragement and support have been the backbone of this endeavour. Without your collective efforts, this book would not have come to fruition, and for that, I am deeply grateful.

Table of Contents

Introduction

Who is this book for?

This book is designed for anyone using Dragon who wants to create practical voice commands to perform application tasks. It is ideal for those beginning their journey into the world of voice command creation, as Step-by-Step commands provide an excellent gateway to exploring the full potential of Dragon.

Although the primary aim of this book is to provide newcomers to Dragon Professional command creation with a comprehensive resource of Dragon Step-by-Step commands to draw on, it also has a secondary goal: to help you progress to the next level by creating your own voice commands. To support this, the commands are thoroughly documented and explained in detail, with guidance provided for many on how to adapt them to your specific requirements.

I hope that by reading through the explanations, rather than simply incorporating the commands into your projects, you'll pick up valuable tips and tricks that many Dragon users take years to discover. By doing so, you'll gain a deeper understanding of creating Dragon voice commands.

To maximise the value of this book, it is assumed that you are already familiar with basic dictation and a range of Dragon's built-in voice commands. Ideally, users will have experience with fundamental voice commands such as "*open microsoft word*" (to open the MS Word application), "*go to sleep*" (to place the microphone into standby), and various commands for formatting and saving documents.

Which version of Dragon is required?

If you are using Dragon NaturallySpeaking Version 13 or earlier, you will need the Professional, Medical, or Legal editions to fully utilise features such as inputting, exporting, and creating Dragon commands. Starting with Version 14, users of Dragon Professional, Dragon Professional Individual, and Dragon Professional Group can utilise the commands discussed in this book.

While the Step-by-Step commands have been created and tested with Dragon Professional 16, users of Dragon Medical One will also find this resource valuable. Although the interface in Dragon Medical One has a slightly different appearance, these commands can be easily adapted and translated into Step-by-Step voice commands for its users.

Screenshots are from Dragon Professional 16, and the instructions for navigating and selecting options within the DragonBar are also based on version 16. While the same instructions can be followed in other versions of Dragon, some options may be located in different places.

What does this book cover?

As the title suggests, the primary purpose of this book is to provide practical and thought-provoking examples of Dragon Step-by-Step commands designed to work across various applications and environments.

Many of the commands in this book showcase scenarios where automation can play a major part in improving productivity or simply carrying out repetitive tasks on your behalf. Each command is supported with a working solution that can be implemented as is or used as a springboard to your own creativity.

This book is divided into 14 sections and to give you an overall picture, here is a summary:

Section 1, "Dragon Command Types" - This section introduces the various types of Dragon commands, the scenarios in which they are useful, and how to create them.

Section 2, "Delving into Step-by-Step Commands" – This section guides you through the process of creating and editing both Step-by-Step and Step-by-Step List commands. It also provides a detailed explanation of the available steps that can be used to construct Step-by-Step commands.

Section 3, "Working with the Step-by-Step Commands in this book" – In this section, you will find a guide on how to interpret the Step-by-Step commands found in this book. You will also find information on how to import Dragon and Dragon List commands, how to update Application-specific commands, and how to train Dragon to recognise your dictated command phrases.

Sections 4 - 13, "101 Ready to use Step-by-Step Dragon commands" - This is the core section of the book. You will find commands that automate popular Office applications such as MS Word, MS Outlook, and MS Excel, as well as commands for MindManager, browsers, Adobe Photoshop, and others. These commands are ready to use and represent real-life scenarios.

Section 14, "Appendix" - The Appendix includes examples of Send Keys Step codes, and the Index.

How to use this book

This book is written in the style of a typical tips guide, with each section demonstrating how Dragon voice commands can be used to perform everyday tasks across various applications. Use this book as a resource for discovering commands that solve common problems, eliminate repetitive tasks, and reduce mouse and keyboard actions. Most importantly, dive into the example commands, skim through them, and start using them right away. Even better, use these examples as a springboard to create your own custom commands tailored to your unique needs.

Note that as applications develop and add features, the steps required or keyboard shortcuts available may change. It is important to test the commands on test documents to ensure they work as expected.

Conventions used in this book

Below you will find the typographical conventions used in this book.

The terms 'macro', 'command', 'custom command', 'recipe', 'script', 'code' and 'voice command' are all interchangeable.

The terms 'Dragon', 'Dragon Professional', 'Dragon Professional Individual (DPI)', 'Dragon Professional Group (DPG)', 'Dragon NaturallySpeaking (DNS)' are all interchangeable.

The terms 'Visual Basic for Applications', 'Application Visual Basic', 'Visual Basic', 'VBA' are all interchangeable.

The steps to access menu options may be written using the following format: The ">>" symbol indicates the path for selecting an item from the DragonBar or application menu. For example, the line "**DragonBar >> Tools >> Command Center**" means you should click on the "Tools" icon in the DragonBar and then select the "Command Browser" from the list of available options. Figure 0-1 shows the DragonBar.

Figure 0-1

The plus sign (+) is used to indicate the pressing of keyboard key combinations, here are some examples:

- Pressing **Ctrl+Shift+F5** means that you should hold down the **Ctrl** key, **Shift** key, then press the **F5** key.
- Pressing **Alt+PrtSc** means you should hold down the **Alt** key and then press the **PrtSc** key.
- A line with **Ctrl+V, W** means to press and hold down the **Ctrl** key, press the **V** key, release the **Ctrl** key and then press the **W** key once.

At times, keyboard combinations will be represented without the plus sign (+). For example, **Alt, N, H** means to press and release the **Alt** key, press and release the **N** key, and then press and release the **H** key.

"*text written in italics and within quotes*" is used to represent something you should say.

Codetypeface indicates actual Dragon code.

Straight quotes must be used within Dragon code (" ").

Curly and single quotes are used elsewhere for descriptive purposes (' ') (" ").

> Throughout this book, you will often see additional note sections. These provide extra information such as warnings, tips, pitfalls, alternatives, and what can and cannot be done in relation to the topic being discussed.

Commands Usage and Licensing

This book serves as a guide, a source of reference, and a tool for experimenting with Dragon application software, enabling you to push its capabilities further than before. I encourage you to try out the command examples and modify them to suit your needs. You do not need to contact me for permission unless you are reproducing a significant portion of the code. For instance, writing a program that incorporates several chunks of code from this book does not require permission. However, selling or distributing a CD-ROM, memory stick, or downloadable file does require permission. Answering a question by citing this book and quoting an example code does not require permission. Incorporating a significant amount of the example code from this book into your products or documentation does require permission.

You are free to use any of the commands in this book in your own projects and may modify them as necessary without attributing this book—although attribution is always appreciated. However, you may not sell, give away, or otherwise distribute the commands themselves in any manner, whether printed or in electronic format, without the written permission of the publisher.

The Companion Website

This book is packed with multiple code examples. To save yourself countless hours and debugging headaches, download the appropriate section commands from this book's companion website at:

dragonspeechtips.com/dp-101-step-commands/

Each command in this book has an associated sample file, which can be found within a downloadable section zip file, allowing you to avoid manually constructing the commands from scratch.

Section 1: Introduction to Dragon Commands and Their Types

This section of the book introduces Dragon commands, explores the different types of commands available, and explains how to create them. It also provides the essential understanding needed to work with the 101 Dragon Step-by-Step commands included in this book.

Dragon commands (also referred to as Dragon Macros) enable us to automate just about any routine or repetitive task on our PCs, and the good news is, you do not need to be a programming expert to create your own bespoke Dragon voice commands. Therefore, if you find yourself clicking the same buttons in the same order multiple times a day, consider creating a voice command to streamline the process and save time.

Dragon commands consist of a set of instructions that direct an application (such as MS Word or MS Excel) to carry out specific tasks to achieve a desired outcome.

Creating your own commands can be extremely beneficial and satisfying. Here are just a few reasons why:

- They can perform complicated sequences that may be difficult to remember; prone to human error; time-consuming or tedious.
- Sufferers of RSI who struggle with using the keyboard and mouse can use Dragon commands to control their PCs in multiple ways.
- For those who struggle with remembering keyboard shortcuts, creating a memorable voice command is far easier than having to remember the keystrokes required.

There is no doubt that creating your own commands will allow you to easily accomplish more in less time. They will carry out your instructions to the letter; perform repetitive tasks flawlessly and in most cases execute tasks a lot faster than a human can.

Dragon allows us to create four types of commands:

- Auto-Text(Text and Graphics)
- Macro Recorder
- Step-by-Step
- Advanced Scripting

The types of commands you can create depend on your version of Dragon. For instance, in Dragon Professional version 16, your options may be limited by how the software was installed. Additionally, some command types might not be immediately visible and may require enabling through the Administrative Settings. To do this, open the DragonBar, click on Settings, select Administrative Settings, go to the Miscellaneous tab, and enable the desired command types.

The type of Dragon command you will want to create depends on its intended function. Table 1-1 offers a basic guide.

Table 1-1

What you want it to do:	Appropriate Command Type to create:
Insert a large amount of text such as a business letter template. Produce some text and/or graphics, such as an email signature with a logo.	Auto-Text(Text and Graphics).
Perform a set of keyboard keystroke actions. Open a specific application and carry out keyboard shortcuts. Open a specific website page in the browser.	Step-by-Step Advanced Scripting.
Fully manipulate an application to perform several tasks. Perform a created application VBA macro. Create a custom user interface or Dialog form.	Advanced Scripting.
Move the mouse, click and perform keystrokes	Advanced Scripting Macro Recorder

Creating Dragon Commands

All command types can be created by either clicking on the DragonBar; clicking on the Tools option, selecting the Command Center and then clicking the Add New Command option. Alternatively, you can turn on the microphone and dictate the command phrase "*add new command*". Both methods will reveal the MyCommands Editor window (see Figure 1-0), ready for you to create a command.

Figure 1-0

The DragonBar

The MyCommands Editor window

The options available to you in the MyCommands Editor window will depend on the type of command you intend to create. To specify the command type, click the **Command Type** drop-down menu and choose from one of the four options (see Figure 1-1).

Figure 1-1

Selecting one of the four Command Types in the MyCommands Editor window.

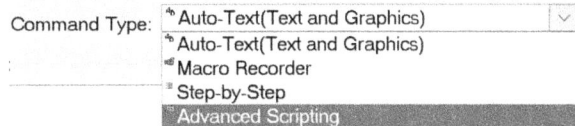

Some of the options available remain constant:

MyCommand Name: This is the actual name you give to a command. It is also the phrase you say to execute the command, for example, "autofit cell width" The exception is when the command you have created includes List Variables, indicated by the use of <...> in the MyCommand Name. In the case of Dragon List commands, the command phrases that you can dictate will be determined by the List items/variables.

Description: This is an optional choice; it allows you to insert a description of what your command will do.

Group: Allows you to have your new command as part of an existing set/group of commands or create a new group. Placing your commands in groups is an ideal way to maintain good file management.

Availability: Commands can be created to run only under certain conditions:

- **Global:** The command can be executed at any time, regardless of the application or environment you are working in.
- **Application-specific:** The command will only execute when you are working within a specific application. When this option is selected, Dragon reveals additional options in the MyCommands Editor, most importantly requiring you to specify the application the command will work with.
- **Window-specific:** The command will only execute when you are working within a specific window of a specified application. When this option is selected, Dragon reveals additional options in the MyCommands Editor.

Auto-Text(Text and Graphics) Commands

Auto-Text(Text and Graphics) commands are essentially the preferred method for inserting unlimited formatted text (with or without images) into your documents.

Auto-Text commands can be used to create email signatures, letter templates and fillable forms - by dictating the command name, the entire text will appear in your documents. They can also be used to quickly insert often used phrases, quotes or sentences.

To create an Auto-Text command: Click on the **DragonBar**, click the **Tools** option, select **Command Center**, and click **Add New Command**, or do the same by saying "*add new command*", both methods will reveal the **MyCommands Editor** window.

In the **MyCommands Editor** window click on the **Command Type** drop-down menu and select the option **Auto-Text(Text and Graphics)**. You can either paste formatted text and images into the Content area or type your text directly into it and use the available options to format or style the text. Figure 1-2 shows an example of an Auto-Text(Text and Graphics) command.

Figure 1-2

An example of an Auto-Text(Text and Graphics) command, consisting of text, an image and fields.

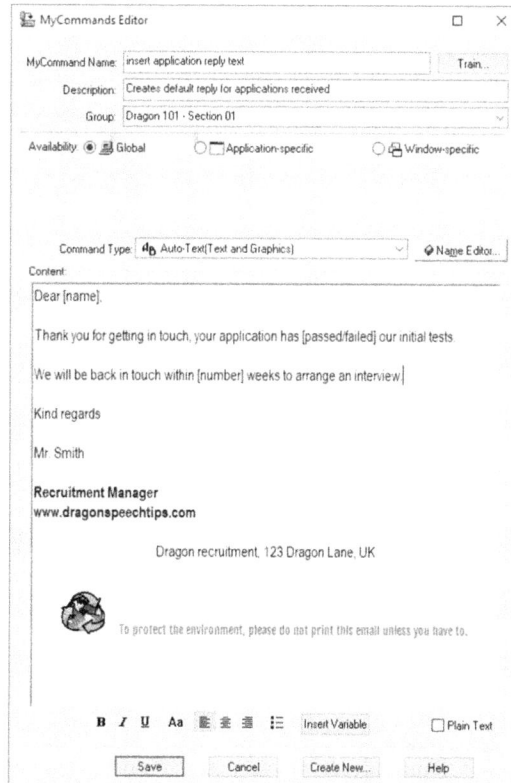

Macro Recorder Commands

Dragon Macro Recorder commands are commands that have been created by recording all the manual steps, including mouse actions that have been carried out to perform a task.

To create a Macro Recorder command, click the **Record** button. Dragon will then record all your mouse movements, mouse clicks and keyboard entries. The information gathered is then used to generate and populate the **Actions** area in the **MyCommands Editor** window (see Figure 1-3), resulting in a list of instructions that Dragon will carry out to perform the task when the command is run.

Figure 1-3

An example of a Macro Recorder type command. It will perform the clicking of the left mouse button and perform cursor movement around the screen.

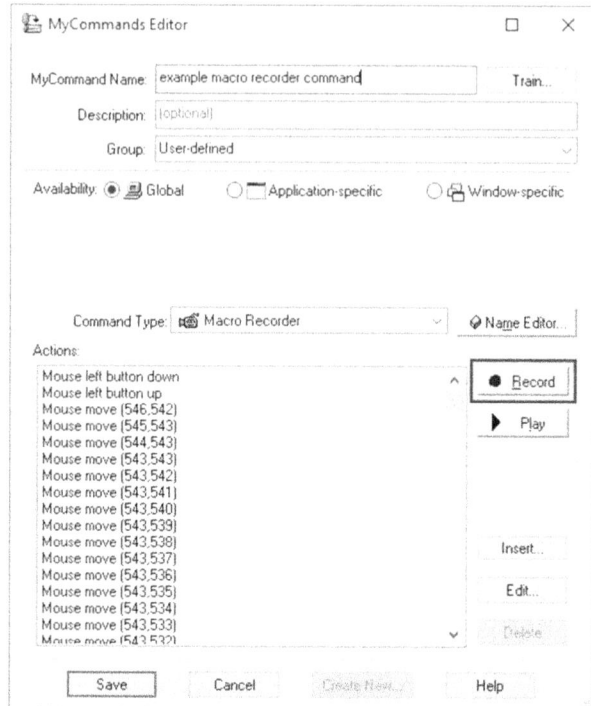

These types of commands often include a significant amount of detail, such as the exact screen coordinate values of the mouse position throughout the process. Personally, I avoid creating Dragon Macro Recorder commands because they tend to be the slowest among the command types and often yield unreliable results, particularly when sharing commands with others.

Step-by-Step Commands

Step-by-Step commands are an excellent introductory method for creating voice commands that will instruct applications to perform specific functions. Even users with no coding experience can quickly create effective commands to execute shortcut keystrokes, open a browser to a specific web page (URL), load specific documents for editing, and more.

While Step-by-Step commands are efficient and effective, more experienced users may prefer creating Advanced Scripting commands to carry out tasks. Advanced Scripting commands execute faster and offer greater flexibility and power for complex automation tasks.

To create a Step-by-Step command: Click on the **DragonBar**, click the **Tools** option, select **Command Center,** and click **Add New Command**. Alternatively, you can achieve the same result by saying "*add new command*", either method will open the **MyCommands Editor** window.

In the **MyCommands Editor** window click on the **Command Type** drop-down menu and select the option **Step-by-Step**.

It is the **Steps** area that will be populated with the list of steps you require the command to perform.

To insert the required steps in the **MyCommands Editor** window:

- Click on the **New Step** drop-down menu and select one of the options.
- Click on the **Insert** button to reveal the properties window of the selected option and insert the necessary details.

The **Move Up** and **Move Down** buttons enable you to re-order (a selected step) your list of steps, and of course, the order is of paramount importance. Figure 1-4 shows an example of a Step-by-Step command, which when run within Microsoft Word will change the page size dimensions to A5.

Figure 1-4

An example of an Application-specific Step-by-Step command. The command will only run when using the MS Word application.

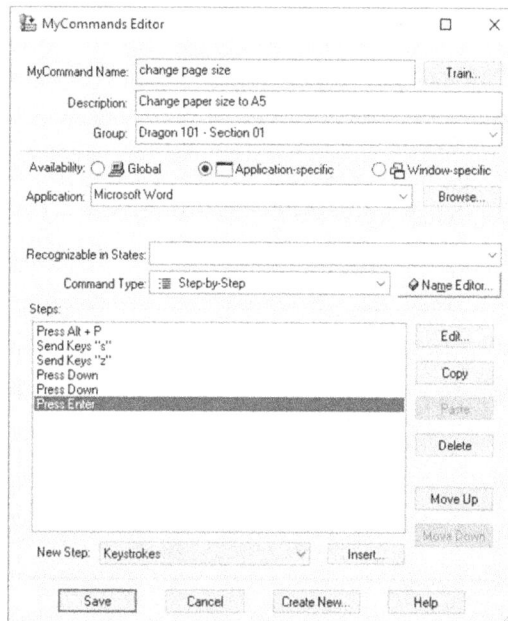

Step-by-Step commands can include Dragon Lists.
Refer to Section 2: Creating Step-by-Step List (List Variables) Commands.

Advanced Scripting Commands

Advanced Scripting commands are the most powerful and effective of all the command types, offering several significant advantages:

- **Speed and Efficiency:** Dragon executes Advanced Scripting commands significantly faster than equivalent Step-by-Step commands.
- **Enhanced Functionality:** These commands can incorporate Dragon Script and VBA code, enabling greater control and automation of your PC compared to other command types.
- **Application Automation:** Advanced Scripting allows for seamless automation and manipulation of applications like Microsoft Word and Excel by integrating application-specific VBA code into Dragon commands.
- **Interactive Dialog Forms:** Advanced Scripting supports the creation of dialog forms, which enable user interaction. These forms can be used to gather and process information in a variety of ways, enhancing the versatility of your commands.

To create an Advanced Scripting command: Click on the **DragonBar**, click the **Tools** option, select **Command Center**, and click **Add New Command**, or do the same by saying "*add new command*". Both methods will reveal the MyCommands Editor window.

In the **MyCommands Editor** window click on the **Command Type** drop-down menu and select the option **Advanced Scripting**.

Any Dragon script or VBA code required to perform the command is inserted between the lines `Sub Main` and `End Sub`. Figure 1.5 shows an example of an Advanced Scripting command containing Dragon Script, that when run, produces a simple Dialog Form.

Figure 1-5

An example of an Advanced Scripting command. It is made up of Dragon script and produces a Dialog Form when run.

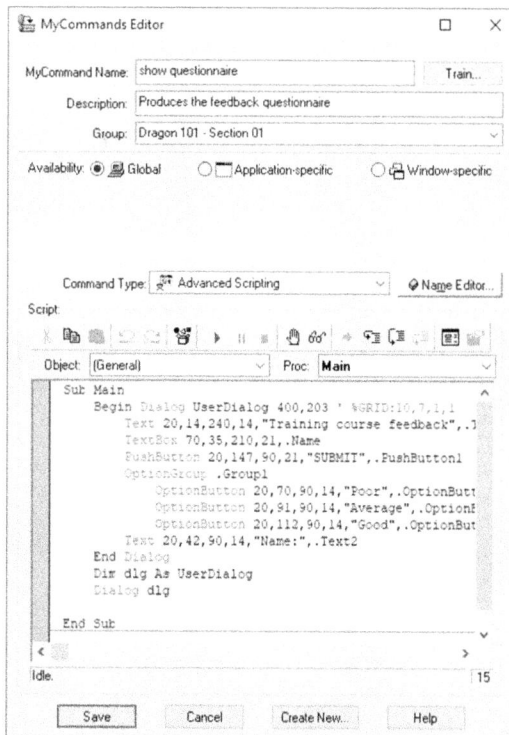

The ability to create Advanced Scripting commands unlocks the full potential of what you can achieve by voice with Dragon, making it an invaluable skill for power users. For a deeper understanding of Advanced Scripting, consider exploring the book *Dragon Professional – A Step Further* (ISBN: 978-1916045040).

Section 2: Delving into Step-by-Step Commands

Creating Step-by-Step Commands

In this section of the book, I will walk you through the thinking and processes required to create Step-by-Step commands; and trust me! There is no greater feeling than the sense of achievement when producing your own commands that perform the tasks you require, all by voice.

Let's start by creating a command that when we say, "*go back*", will emulate the pressing of the back button (as can be seen in Figure 2-0) when browsing web pages within the Google Chrome browser.

Figure 2-0

The Google Chrome back button; used to return to the previous web page.

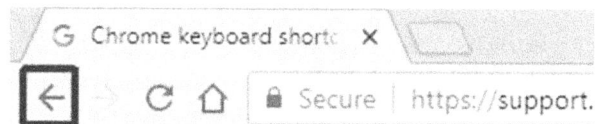

Our approach to this scenario would be to first think about, and answer the following questions:

1. Is there a shortcut keystroke or sequence of keystrokes that will carry out this action when using Chrome? Yes (**Alt+Left arrow**)
2. Do I want this voice command to only work when I am using Google Chrome? Yes
3. Is creating a Step-by-Step type of Dragon command suitable for performing the task? Yes

> The answer to question 1 is easily found by searching the Internet with the question "what is the keyboard shortcut for the back button in Google Chrome?"

Now that we have answered "Yes" to all our questions, let's go through the process of how we put our command together:

First, on the **DragonBar**, click the **Tools** option, select **Command Center**, and click **Add New Command**. Alternatively, you can turn on the Dragon microphone and say, "*add new command*". Both methods will reveal the **MyCommands Editor** window.

Now, let's fill in the fields.

In the **MyCommand Name** field, type in the command name ("go back"). This name will also serve as the command phrase you dictate to Dragon to execute the command.

> It is best practice to write the MyCommand Name in lowercase, unless the command phrase includes an abbreviation.

The **Description** field is optional and allows us to insert a brief description of what our command does.

The **Group** option enables us to either have this command as part of an existing set of commands or create a new group name for the command. For now, let's leave it in the default "User-defined" group of commands.

> A command can be moved to another group at any time.

Next, in the **Availability** section of the window, select the **Application-specific** radio button. This addresses the second question, ensuring that the command is only active and available when browsing within Google Chrome.

By selecting the **Application-specific** option, Dragon will display additional options for configuration. Click on the **Application** drop-down menu to view a list of currently open applications and select **Google Chrome**. If **Google Chrome** does not appear in the list, open the browser, switch back to the **Global** option, then reselect the **Application-specific** option, and check the **Application** drop-down menu again.

> If you still do not see Google Chrome in your list, you will need to click on the Browse button and navigate to the folder containing the Google Chrome executable file (Chrome.exe). Most likely the file can be found in the following path: C:\Program Files\Google\Chrome\Application. Select it and click the Open button. Figure 2-1 shows the path to the file in the Choose Application window.

Figure 2-1

Next, by clicking on the down arrow within the **Command Type** drop-down menu, we can select the type of command we wish to create (**Step-by-Step**), as shown in Figure 2-2.

Figure 2-2

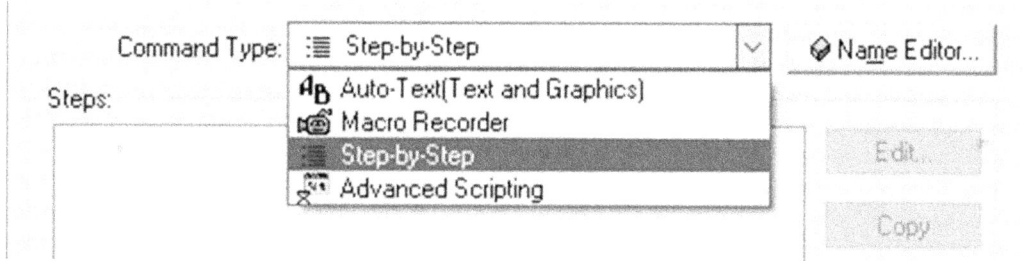

Now, within the **Steps** area, we need to add the Steps that will perform the action we require. To do this, click on **New Step** drop-down menu to reveal several options (see Figure 2-3).

Figure 2-3

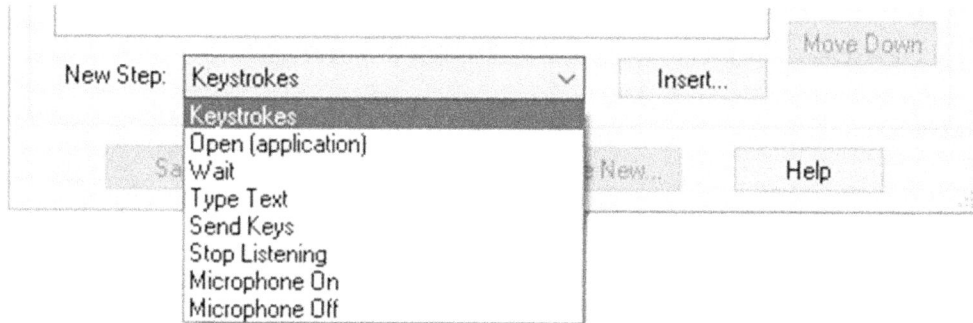

Since performing the action requires pressing the **Alt+Left Arrow** keys, we select **Keystrokes** from the list and click the **Insert** button.

This now presents us with the **Send Keystrokes** window. Click inside the field and perform the keystroke **Alt+Left Arrow** Key. The result should look as shown in Figure 2-4.

Figure 2-4

Perform the required keystroke in the Send Keystrokes window. If you make a mistake, perform the keystroke again and it will overwrite the mistake. Press the OK button to confirm the Step.

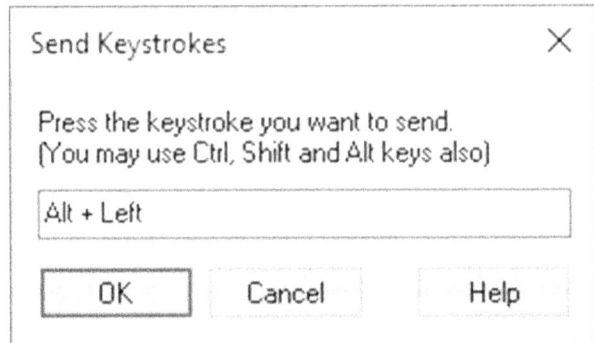

Send Keystrokes ✕

Press the keystroke you want to send.
(You may use Ctrl, Shift and Alt keys also)

Alt + Left

OK   Cancel   Help

Click the **OK** button to close the **Send Keystrokes** window.

That's it! The **MyCommands Editor** window should now look as shown in Figure 2-5.

Figure 2-5

The MyCommands Editor with an Application-specific Step-by-Step command. A created Step is shown in the Steps area.

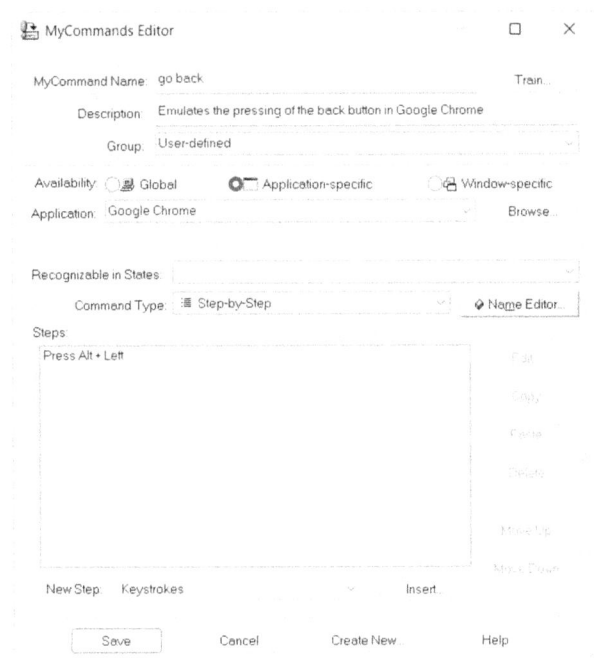

MyCommands Editor   ☐ ✕

MyCommand Name: go back   Train.

Description: Emulates the pressing of the back button in Google Chrome

Group: User-defined

Availability: ◯ Global   ◉ Application-specific   ◯ Window-specific
Application: Google Chrome   Browse

Recognizable in States:

Command Type: Step-by-Step   ◆ Name Editor.

Steps:
Press Alt + Left

New Step: Keystrokes   Insert.

Save   Cancel   Create New   Help

Click the **Save** button to save the new command.

Now, to test the command, open Google Chrome, search through several web pages and when you are ready, try the new command by saying "*go back*".

Discuss

In this scenario, we only needed one set of keystrokes to achieve our objective. There will be times when you might need two or more keystrokes to perform an action. In such instances, the same procedure applies. However, once you have inserted your first keystroke, you will need to click on the Insert button again to insert your second keystroke, and so on. This will eventually build a list of keystrokes in the Steps area.

Let's now look at a second example that involves more steps. Below is a Step-by-Step command consisting of **Keystrokes** and **Wait** steps that will select all the text in an MS Word document, open the Font window, and change the font. Although this may not be the most efficient method, it demonstrates how a Step-by-Step command can be used to carry out a task.

Try it by creating a new Step-by-Step Dragon command and populating the **MyCommand Editor** with the following:

MyCommand Name: make a change to my font

Description:

Group: User-defined

Availability: Application-specific

Application: Microsoft Word

Command Type: Step-by-Step

Steps:

```
Press Ctrl + A
Wait 1000 milliseconds
Press Ctrl + D
Wait 1000 milliseconds
Press Down
Press Down
Press Down
Press Up
Press Down
Press Enter
```

To insert the Wait 1000 milliseconds step, click on the New Step drop-down menu and select Wait, click on the Insert button, adjust the timescale to 1000 in the revealed Wait Step window and click OK.

The steps Press Down and Press Up are achieved by pressing the keyboard down/up arrows keys in the Send Keystrokes window.
The step Press Enter is achieved by pressing Enter in the Send Keystrokes window.

The order of the Steps is important to achieve the desired result. To rearrange the order of the Steps, select a Step and click either the Move Up or Move Down buttons to rearrange the order.

Now try the command by opening MS Word, type in some text and then say, "*make a change to my font*".

Discuss

In this scenario, the first step is to perform Press Ctrl-A, which is the keyboard shortcut to select everything in the Word document.

The Wait 1000 milliseconds step is used to pause the command for one second before moving onto the next step.

The step Press Ctrl-D within MS Word will open the Font window.

The second **Wait** step is used to allow time for the Font window to open before moving onto the Keystroke steps of Press Down and Press Up. These emulate the pressing of the up and down keyboard arrow keys.

Finally Press Enter is the step which tells Dragon to press the **Enter** key, which will close the Font window and change the font of the text within the document.

When creating Step-by-Step commands, think about the logical order of keyboard sequences needed to achieve a task. Practice the steps by keyboard first; sometimes you will need to use a Wait step to slow down the speed of the command, to allow an application to keep up.

Editing Step-by-Step Commands

All your created commands, including imported ones, can be accessed through the **Command Browser –
MyCommands** window.

To open it, navigate to **DragonBar >> Tools >> Command Center >> Command Browser**, or simply say,
"*open command browser*".

Once in the Command Browser, locate your command within the appropriate group and double-click it to
open it in the **MyCommands Editor** window.

When editing Step-by-Step commands, Dragon provides several button options within the MyCommands
Editor:

Edit button: Select a step and click the Edit button to open the pop-up window for that step, allowing you to
modify its settings, text, or code.

Copy button: Use the Copy button to duplicate a selected step along with its properties.

Paste button: Use the Paste button to insert the copied step into a different position in the sequence.

Delete button: Click the Delete button to remove the selected step.

Move Up / Move Down buttons: Use these buttons to adjust the order of steps by moving the selected step up
or down in the sequence.

Figure 2-6

The MyCommands Editor window displaying the
available editing options for a Step-by-Step command.

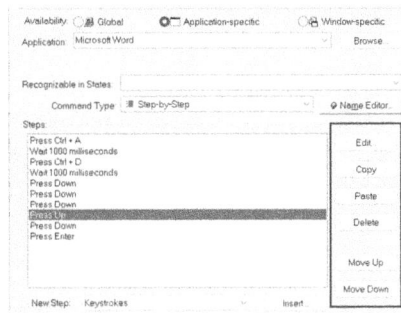

Exploring the available Steps that can be used when creating Step-by-Step commands

As the name suggests, a Step-by-Step command consists of a series of sequenced instructions (steps) that Dragon executes one after the other. For many users, Step-by-Step commands are a preferred way to emulate keyboard shortcuts within applications.

When creating Step-by-Step commands, you will need to choose from the available steps that provide the means by which you can instruct Dragon to perform specific tasks (see Figure 2-7).

Figure 2-7

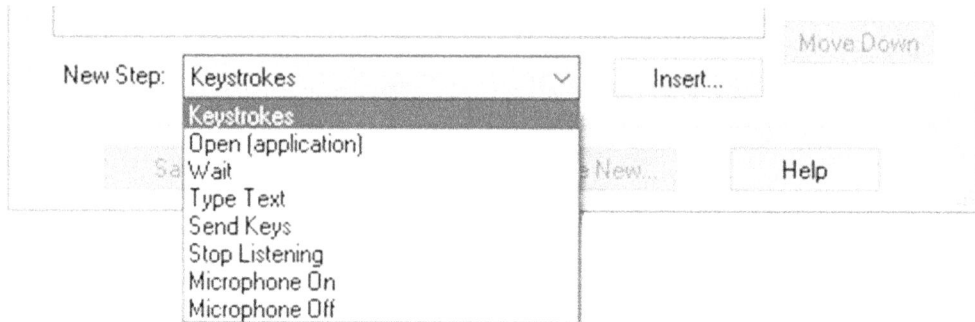

Below is an overview of the various **New Step** options available to you when creating Step-by-Step commands:

Keystrokes:

Figure 2-8

An example keystroke combination in the Send Keystrokes window.

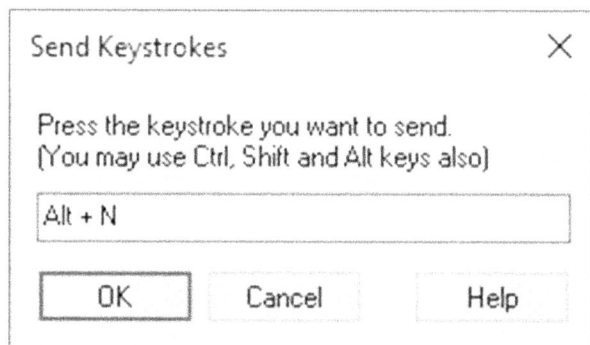

The Keystroke option is used when we want Dragon to perform the pressing of a specific keystroke or keystrokes combination. Once you have selected Keystrokes and clicked on the Insert button, the Send Keystrokes window will appear.

Place the cursor in the blank field and carry out the keystroke. If you make a mistake, just carry out the keystroke again and it will overwrite the mistake. Figure 2-8 shows an example keystroke combination in the Send Keystrokes window.

Examples of keystrokes include: `Press Alt + B`, `Press Ctrl + B`, `Press Enter`, `Press Escape` and `Press Tab`.

Open (application):

Figure 2-9

The Open Application / Document Step window. Inserted in the Target field is the directory path to the file to be opened.

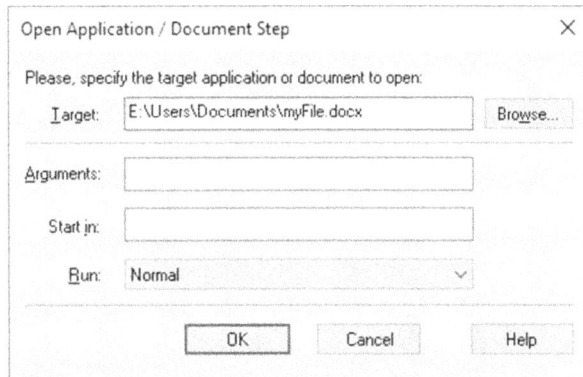

Open Application / Document Step		✕
Please, specify the target application or document to open:		
_T_arget: `E:\Users\Documents\myFile.docx`		Bro_w_se...
_A_rguments:		
Start _i_n:		
_R_un: Normal ⌄		
	OK Cancel Help	

The Open (application) step is used when you want Dragon to open a specific application, document, or navigate to a specific URL. If the document or application is already open, Dragon will switch to it.

The Open Application / Document Step window (see Figure 2-9) includes several parameters:

Target field: This is where you can paste a link to a specific URL or type the name of an application you want to open, such as Notepad, Chrome, Firefox, or Msedge.

To open a specific document or an application that Dragon doesn't recognise, click the **Browse** button. This will bring up the **Choose Application or Document** window. From there, navigate to the folder where your document or application's executable file is located, and click **Open**.

> If the Target field is greyed out, you will need to click on the Browse button and navigate to the specific document or application executable file.

Arguments: This field is used when additional information is required. For example, if you have entered 'Chrome' in the Target field and want a specific web page to open in the Chrome browser, you would enter the full URL of the page into the Arguments field.

Start in: Usually Dragon will automatically supply this information. It refers to the Directory in which the application or document should open.

Run: Determines the window mode in which the application will run:

- Normal
- Minimized
- Maximized

Wait:

Figure 2-10

You can pause the flow of a command by adjusting the wait time in the Wait Step window.

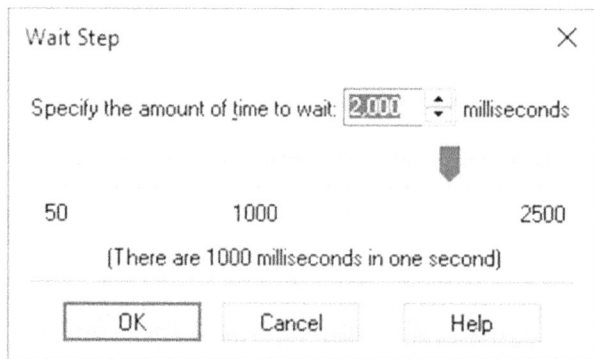

Use the Wait step to pause a command for a specific amount of time, delaying the process from moving to the next step. For example, if the previous step opens an application or document, including a Wait step on the next line ensures there is enough time for it to fully open before proceeding to the next step, which might be to populate it with data. Figure 2-10 shows the Wait Step window.

Type Text:

Figure 2-11

The Type Text Step window. Insert the text you want Dragon to type out.

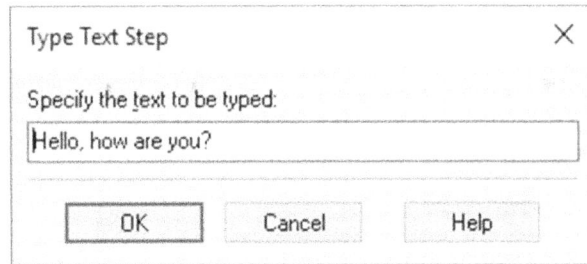

> **Type Text Step**   ✕
>
> Specify the text to be typed:
>
> | Hello, how are you? |
>
>   OK   Cancel   Help

Use the Type Text step to have Dragon type out the text you specify in the field (see Figure 2-11). For example, you might want your command to populate a field in a form with specific text.

☞ There is a limit of 260 characters that can be inserted, and paragraph breaks are not allowed.

☞ You can only use alphanumeric characters found on the keyboard.

Send Keys:

Figure 2-12

The Send Keys Step window. Specify the key sequence you want Dragon to perform.

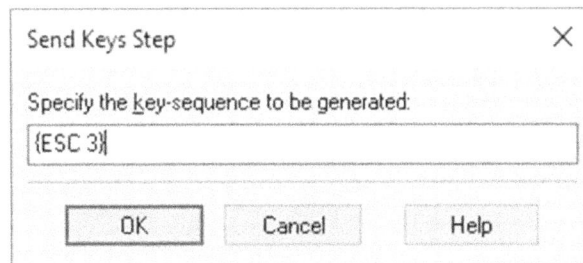

> **Send Keys Step**   ✕
>
> Specify the key-sequence to be generated:
>
> | {ESC 3} |
>
>   OK   Cancel   Help

The Send Keys step is used to perform a sequence of keys (see Figure 2-12). For example, if you want your command to press the Tab button five times, you can do this by inserting {Tab 5}. There are several Send Keys codes available, such as {LBUTTON} to press the left mouse button and {RBUTTON} to press the right mouse button.

> When entering text in the "Send Keys" step, ensure you include a space after the code and before the value, such as in {ESC 3}.

The CTRL, SHIFT and ALT modifier key sequences can also be included. For example, to press Shift+Tab twice, you would insert +{Tab 2}. Table 2-0 shows the symbols used to include Ctrl, Shift and Alt in a Step.

Table 2-0

Ctrl+Tab is written as:	^{TAB}
Shift+Tab is written as:	+{TAB}
Alt+Tab is written as:	%{TAB}

For a list of the Send Keys codes, see the Appendix, *Send Keys Step Code Reference Table*.

Stop Listening:

By including the Stop Listening step, Dragon will place the microphone into sleep (standby) mode when it reaches this line.

Microphone On:

By including the Microphone On step, Dragon will turn on the microphone when it reaches this line in the order of steps.

Microphone Off:

By including the Microphone Off step, Dragon will turn off the microphone when it reaches this line in the order of steps. This step is useful when you want to ensure that the command is carried out without any interruptions, which may occur if a user speaks during the process.

Creating Step-by-Step List (List Variables) Commands

Creating Step-by-Step List commands will enable you to create commands that allow you to dictate multiple phrases to run the same command. For example, imagine you've created a Step-by-Step command named "open client template" that opens a specific Word document. To make it easier and reduce the need to remember the exact command phrase, you can create a Dragon List with the following options:

- "open the client template"
- "open template"
- "new client document"

By creating this Dragon List, you will now be able to dictate any of the phrases to execute the same command.

Creating a Dragon List

To create a Dragon List command, open the **MyCommands window** and place the cursor in the **MyCommand Name** field. Type in the less than (<) sign. You will notice that as soon as you type the less-than sign (angle bracket), Dragon switches you to the **MyCommands Name Editor** window (see figure 2-13).

Figure 2-13

The MyCommands Name Editor window, showing a less-than sign (angle bracket) in the MyCommand Name field.

Type the List name enclosed in angle brackets (<List name>) into the **MyCommand Name** field. For example, "`<open_template>`". The less than (<) and greater than (>) signs are important and tell Dragon we are creating a List variable.

Once the name of the List is enclosed with a greater-than sign, select the List to enable the Edit button (see figure 2-14).

Figure 2-14

The MyCommands Name Editor interface, showing the List "open_template".

You can name your List variable as you prefer, using letters, numbers and underscore (_) characters. However, the name must use only lowercase letters, and spaces are not allowed.

Click the **Edit** button to reveal the **View List** window and insert the list of phrases you want to be able to execute the command (see figure 2-15).

Figure 2-15

The View List window, showing the list of phrases.

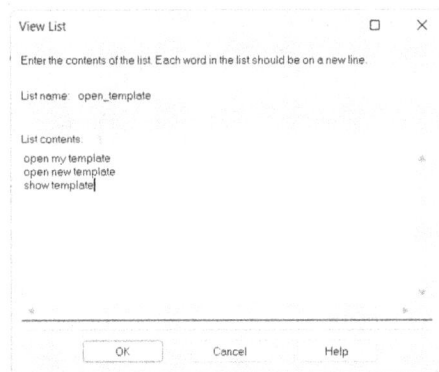

> Points to consider when creating Dragon Lists:
> * A List must consist of 1 or more entries.
> * Each entry within a List can be a single word or phrase.
> * Each entry must be on a separate line.

Click **OK** to finish and return to the **MyCommands Name Editor** window.

Click **OK** to return to the **MyCommands Editor** window.

Dragon List Commands and Advanced Scripting.

Dragon List commands are a powerful tool that can play an integral role in creating Advanced Scripting commands. By incorporating Dragon Lists into Advanced Scripting, you unlock a wide range of possibilities for creating complex commands that adapt based on what the user dictates.

In addition to their versatility, Dragon Lists can significantly simplify scripts by reducing the need for extensive If-Then statements, making your commands more efficient and easier to manage.

For an in-depth exploration of the power and potential of Dragon Lists within Advanced Scripting commands, see *Dragon Professional – A Step Further* (ISBN: 978-1916045040).

Editing Step-by-Step List Commands

There may be times when you need to update a List variable, either by adding new items or removing existing ones. This could be because you frequently dictate a command phrase that wasn't originally included, or because some items in the List are no longer appropriate for executing the specific command.

Editing Dragon Lists

To edit the list of items within a Dragon List Variable. For example, to modify the command <open_client_template_form> and update its Dragon List Variable, proceed as follows:

- Double click the command in the **Command Browser** to reveal it in the **MyCommands Editor** window.
- In the **MyCommands Editor** window click the **Name Editor** button to reveal the **MyCommands Name Editor** window, as shown in Figure 2-16.

Figure 2-16

The MyCommands Name Editor window displays a list Dragon Lists used in the command.

To edit the items in a Dragon List, select it from the Lists used in this command section and click the Edit button.

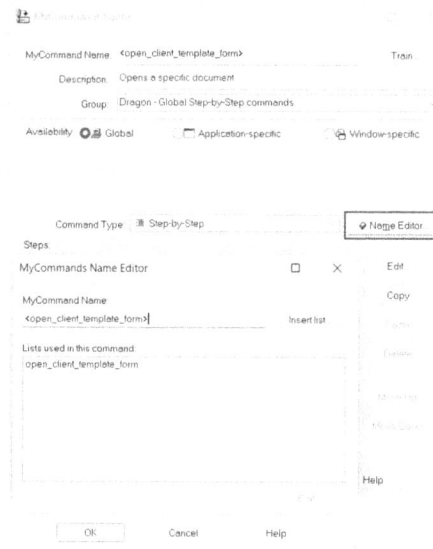

- Select the List "open_client_template_form" and click the **Edit** button to reveal the **View List** window (see Figure 2-17).

Figure 2-17

The View List window displays the items of a selected Dragon List. You can add, edit or delete items.

All items must be inserted on separate lines.

The order of the items is not important and will be automatically sorted into alphabetical order.

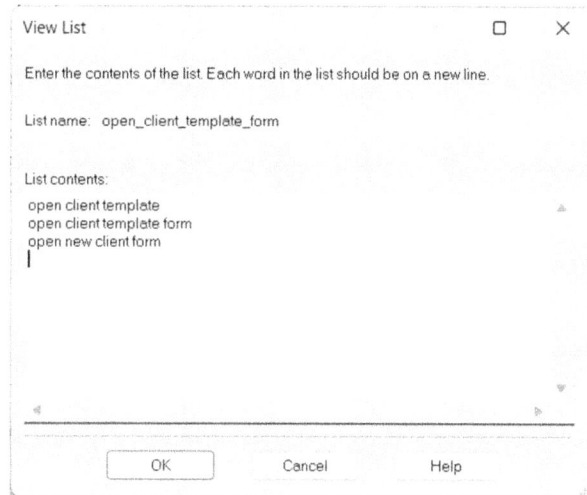

View List	□	×

Enter the contents of the list. Each word in the list should be on a new line.

List name: open_client_template_form

List contents:

open client template
open client template form
open new client form

OK	Cancel	Help

- Edit the list of items and click **OK**.
- Click **OK** to close the **MyCommands Name Editor** window.
- Click **Save** to close the **MyCommands Editor** window.

Section 3: Working with the Step-by-Step Commands in this book

Using the Command Examples

Most of the 101 Step-by-Step commands in this book follow a simple structure:

- Scenario
- Solution
- Discussion

Each command is detailed using the following components:

MyCommand name: The suggested name for the command. You can rename it to suit your preference.

Name of List(s) used: The name(s) of the List(s) included in the command.

List items: Displays the items contained within the List(s).

Description: Outlines the purpose of the command (optional).

Group: Indicates the Group to which the command belongs, as shown in the Command Browser.

Availability: Specifies the command type—**Global** (can be run in any environment), **Application-specific** (will only run when working within a specified application), or **Window-specific** (will only work within a specified window in a specific application).

Application: Shows the application in which the command will work (only shown when the **Availability** option is not set to **Global**).

Command Type: Identifies the type of command: Auto-Text(Text and Graphics), Macro Recorder, Step-by-Step, or Advanced Scripting.

Steps: Provides the sequential Step(s) required to perform the command.

Try it by saying: Lists the word, phrase, or example phrases (for commands with Dragon Lists) that can be dictated to execute the command.

> Throughout this book, I have displayed my recommended text and choices for you to use. However, please feel free to change the command name, description, or group name if you wish. Be aware that changing the availability may produce undesired results.

Obtaining the Sample Commands

Each command in this book comes with a sample file, available in a downloadable section zip file, so you won't need to create the commands manually.

Refer to the "The Companion Website" section in this book's Introduction for direction on how to download the sample macros.

Importing the Sample Commands (Macros)

The commands downloaded from the companion site are in the form of .*dat* files.

To import the commands into Dragon, open the **Command Browser** (see Figure 3-0). You can do this by clicking on the **DragonBar**, selecting the **Tools** option, choosing **Command Center**, and then clicking **Command Browser**. Alternatively, turn on the microphone and dictate, "*open command browser*".

Figure 3-0

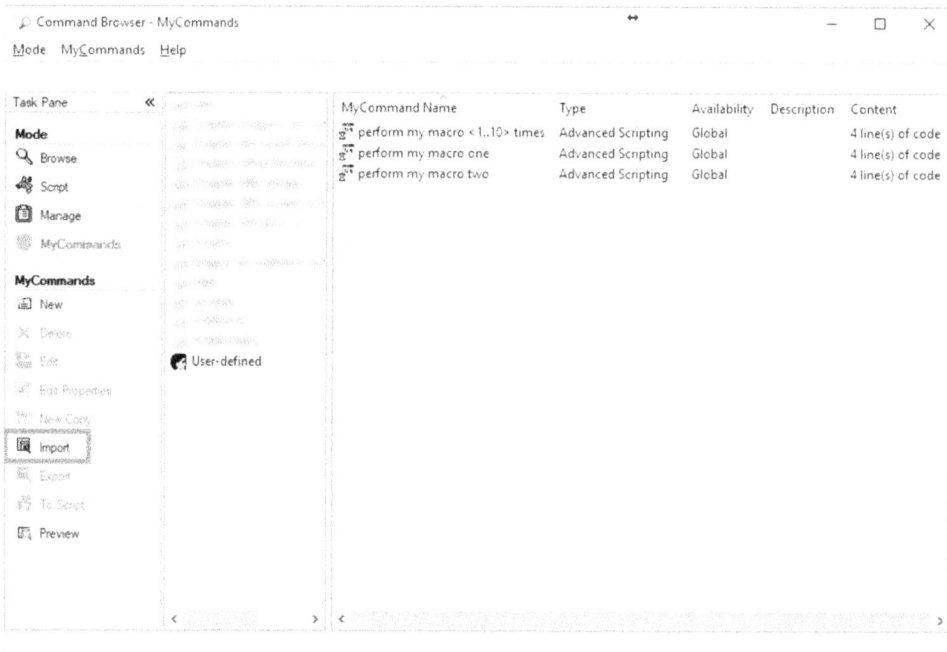

Click the **Import** button on the left-hand side of the **Command Browser** to reveal the **Import Commands window**.

Navigate to the location of the .*dat* file that you wish to import and click the **Open** button. Figure 3-1 shows a selected .*dat* file to be imported.

If your intended file is not visible, ensure that the file type next to the filename field (e.g., 'MyCommands files (.dat)') matches the type of file you want to import. Alternatively, select 'All files (.*)' from the menu. This will display all files and allow you to locate your intended file.

Figure 3-1

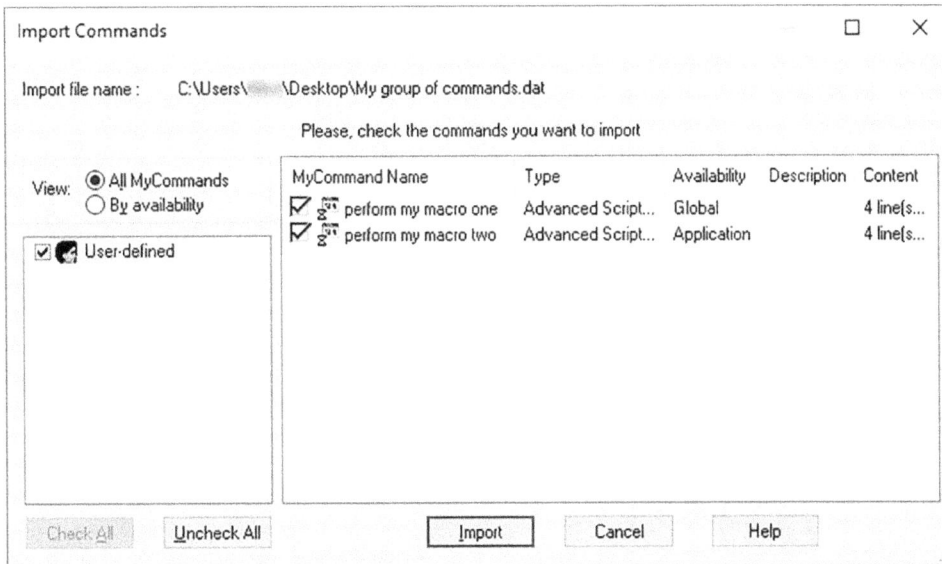

In this scenario, we selected the "My group of commands.dat" file for import. The Import Commands window displays all the commands contained within the *.dat* file.

On the left-hand side of the window, "User-defined" indicates the group (folder) where the commands will be placed.

There are two view options (see Figure 3-2):

Figure 3-2

Selecting one of the two View options when importing Dragon commands.

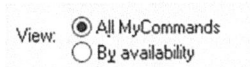

The **All MyCommands** view displays a list of commands contained within the *.dat* file, as shown in Figure 3-1.

The **By Availability** view provides a detailed breakdown of the commands contained within the *.dat* file (as shown in Figure 3-3). This view categorises commands by their availability state: Global, Application-specific, or Window-specific. Clicking on 'Global' will display the commands categorised as Global in the .dat file. Similarly, selecting 'Application-specific' or 'Window-specific' will display the corresponding commands in the right-hand section.

Figure 3-3

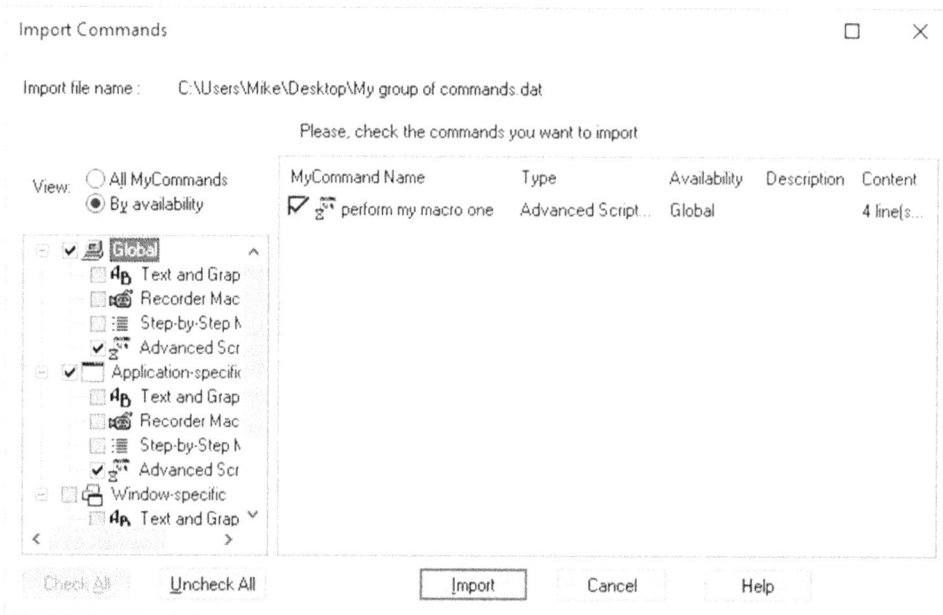

You can now choose to import all the selected macros or only the specific macros you need. Click the **Import** button to complete the process.

☞ Imported commands will be placed in the same group (folder) from which they were originally exported.

☞ If a user imports an Application-specific command but does not have the corresponding application installed on their PC, Dragon will still allow the command to be imported. However, the voice command will not function until the application is installed on the target PC.

Importing Macros that contain Dragon Lists

When importing a command that contains a Dragon List, Dragon automatically imports the List along with its items. However, if a Dragon List with the same name already exists on the end-user's PC, Dragon will display a warning (see Figure 3-4).

Figure 3-4

When a user attempts to import a Dragon command containing a Dragon List, Dragon will check to see if the List name conflicts with an existing List name. If it does, Dragon will display the Import Commands window and prompt the user for confirmation.

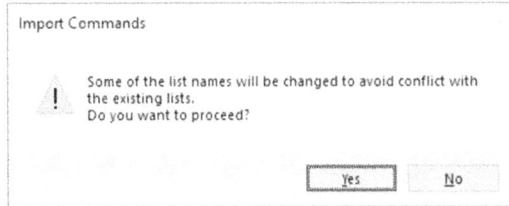

Once you give the go ahead, Dragon will create a newly named version of the List and update the imported command's name to include the new List name.

Updating Application-specific Commands

Application-specific commands may occasionally stop working or fail to function properly after being imported. Possible reasons include:

- The version of the application on your PC differs from the version used when the command was created.
- The application has recently been updated, requiring a newly named executable file to run.
- The application update has created a new folder containing the executable file.

You can resolve these issues for individual commands or multiple commands at once by following these steps:

- Open the **Command Browser** via the **DragonBar** >> **Tools** >> **Command Center** >> **Command Browser**, locate and select the command(s) you wish to change, as shown in Figure 3-5.
- Click on the **Edit** Properties button to reveal the **MyCommands Properties** window (see Figure 3-6).

Figure 3-5

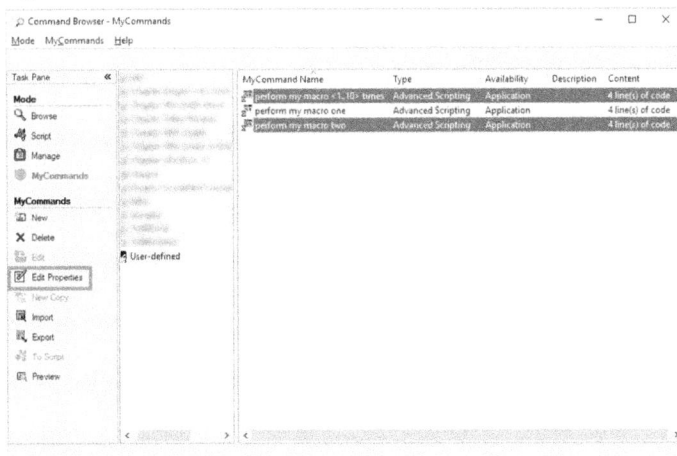

Figure 3-6

You can use the MyCommands Properties window to view and change the command properties of the selected commands.

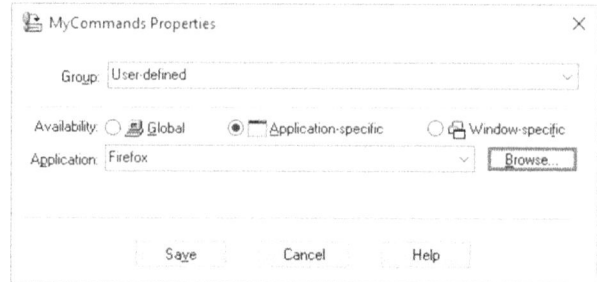

Select the **Application-specific** radio button and click the **Browse** button to locate the new application executable file. Once done, click the **Save** button.

All selected commands will now be updated to the new application version.

Training Dragon to recognise how you pronounce voice commands

Whether you're working with imported macros or commands you've created, there may be times when Dragon fails to recognise or inconsistently executes a voice command you dictate.

In such cases, it's a good idea to train Dragon to recognise how you pronounce the command. Training not only improves Dragon's accuracy but also updates your user profile for better future performance.

To train a voice command (of any type), follow these steps:

- Open the command within the **MyCommands Editor** window (see Figure 3-7).
- Click the **Train** button to reveal the **Train Words** window (see Figure 3-8).

Figure 3-7

Open a command in the MyCommands Editor window and click the Train button to begin the training process.

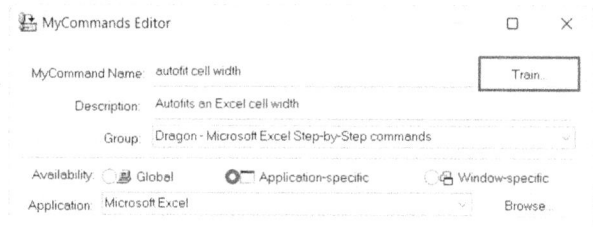

Figure 3-8

The Train Words window displays the word or phrase to be trained. Click the Train button to record your speech and then click the Save button.

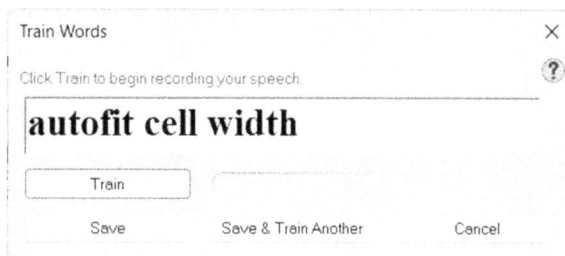

Train Words   ✕

Click Train to begin recording your speech.

autofit cell width

Train

Save   Save & Train Another   Cancel

- Click the **Train** button and dictate the voice command phrase
- Click **Save**.

If your voice command includes a Dragon List(s), as shown in Figure 3-9, the **Train Words** window will allow you to train Dragon for each variation (see Figure 3-10).

Figure 3-9

Open a command containing a Dragon List in the MyCommands Editor window and click the Train button to begin the training process.

MyCommands Editor   ☐ ✕

MyCommand Name: <apply_my_highlight_style>   Train...

Description: Changes the text to my highlighted style

Group: Dragon - Microsoft Word Step-by-Step commands

Availability: ○ Global   ● Application-specific   ○ Window-specific

Application: Microsoft Word   Browse...

Figure 3-10

The Train Words window displays each word or phrase variation and allows the user to train Dragon for each one.

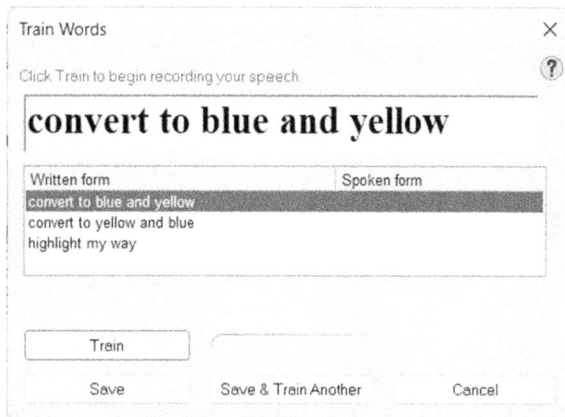

Train Words   ✕

Click Train to begin recording your speech.

convert to blue and yellow

Written form	Spoken form
convert to blue and yellow	
convert to yellow and blue	
highlight my way	

Train

Save   Save & Train Another   Cancel

Where can you go from here?

Whether you are a beginner or an experienced user, I highly recommend the book "Dragon Professional – A Step Further" (ISBN: 978-1916045040) to further enhance your skills in creating Dragon commands. This book covers Dragon command types, the Dragon scripting language, creating Dialog Forms, and much more in an accessible and engaging way. It provides clear, easy-to-follow examples and can also serve as a valuable reference guide.

Most of the macros included in the book leverage Dragon script and Application Visual Basic (VBA) to perform their functions, allowing for the creation of faster and more complex commands.

101 Ready to use Dragon Commands

Section 4: Dragon Global Commands

Dragon Global Commands

In this section, you'll find a collection of **Global Step-by-Step** commands that can help make your workflow faster and more efficient. Since these commands are global, you can use them no matter what application or environment you're working in, giving you more flexibility and convenience.

The commands range from simple browser actions to practical shortcuts that cut down on the need for mouse clicks and keyboard typing. By using these commands, you can save time and reduce the repetitive tasks that slow you down.

These commands aren't included with Dragon by default, but they can easily be created and added to your setup to help improve your productivity and make your day-to-day tasks a lot easier.

In This Part: Step-by-Step Commands 1–20

Automatically Inserting Commas in Currency Amounts Less Than 10,000

Scenario

You frequently work with currency amounts in your documents. However, by default, Dragon only inserts a comma for values over 10,000, meaning for any amount less than 10,000, you have to manually dictate a comma in the correct position. This extra step can be time-consuming and prone to errors.

To save time and streamline your workflow, this **Step-by-Step** command can be used. After dictating the amount, simply say the command "apply currency format", and Dragon automatically inserts the comma in the correct place. The cursor is then returned to its original position, allowing you to continue dictating without any interruptions. This command eliminates the need for manual corrections, making your work more efficient and accurate.

MyCommand Name: apply currency format

Description: Automatically inserts a comma in the correct position for amounts under 10,000

Group: Dragon – Global Step-by-Step commands

Availability: Global

Command Type: Step-by-Step

Steps:

```
Send Keys Send Keys "{Left 3}"
Type Text Type ","
Send Keys Send Keys "{Right 3}"
```

Figure 4-0

The MyCommands Editor window, displaying the configuration for the "apply currency format" command and its required steps.

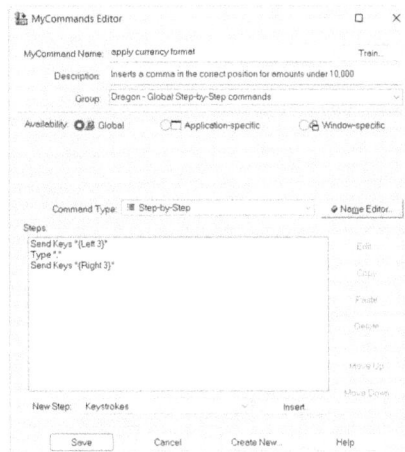

Open a Word document and try it by saying:

"three thousand and fifty dollars" (followed by) *"apply currency format"*

Discuss

This command begins with a Send Keys step to move the cursor three places to the left by emulating the Left Arrow key press three times. Next, a Type Text step inserts the comma, followed by another Send Keys step to move the cursor three places to the right.

> When inserting the text within the "Send Keys" step, it is important to include a space after the code and before the value such as in {Right 3}.

Surrounding the Selected Text with Square Brackets

Dragon provides voice commands such as 'Bracket that' and 'Quote that' to surround the selected text with brackets or quotes. However, there is no default voice command to surround the selected text with square brackets.

This **Step-by-Step** command enables you to do this by dictating the command phrase "Square brackets that" when text is selected.

MyCommand Name: square brackets that

Description: Places square brackets around the selected text

Group: Dragon – Global Step-by-Step commands

Availability: Global

Command Type: Step-by-Step

Steps:

```
Keystrokes Press Ctrl + C
Type Text Type "["
Keystrokes Press Ctrl + V
Type Text Type "]"
Keystrokes Press Right
```

Figure 4-1

The MyCommands Editor window, displaying the configuration for the "square brackets that" command and its required steps.

Open a document, select some text, and try it by saying:
"square brackets that"

Discuss

This command consists of several steps. First, a **Keystrokes** step uses the keyboard shortcut **Ctrl+C** to copy the selected text to the clipboard. Next, a **Type Text** step inserts the **Open Square Bracket** symbol, followed by another **Keystrokes** step to paste the contents of the clipboard. Then, a **Type Text** step inserts the **Close Square Bracket** symbol. Finally, a **Keystrokes** step presses the **Right Arrow** key to position the cursor outside the brackets.

Surrounding the Selected Text with Curly Brackets

Dragon provides voice commands such as 'Bracket that' and 'Quote that' to surround the selected text with brackets or quotes. However, there is no default voice command to surround the selected text with curly brackets.

This **Step-by-Step** command enables you to do this by dictating the command phrase "curly brackets that" when text is selected.

MyCommand Name: curly brackets that

Description: Places curly brackets around the selected text

Group: Dragon – Global Step-by-Step commands

Availability: Global

Command Type: Step-by-Step

Steps:

```
Keystrokes Press Ctrl + C
Type Text Type "{}"
Keystrokes Press Left
Keystrokes Press Ctrl + V
Keystrokes Press Right
```

Figure 4-2

The MyCommands Editor window, displaying the configuration for the "curly brackets that" command and its required steps.

Open a document, select some text, and try it by saying:
"curly brackets that"

Discuss

This command consists of several steps. First, a **Keystrokes** step uses the keyboard shortcut **Ctrl+C** to copy the selected text to the clipboard. Next, a **Type Text** step inserts the **Open and Close Curly Bracket** symbols. A **Keystrokes** step presses the **Left Arrow** key, followed by another **Keystrokes** step to paste the contents of the clipboard. Finally, a **Keystrokes** step presses the **Right Arrow** key to position the cursor outside the brackets.

Enclosing the Selected Text within Vertical Bars

Dragon provides voice commands like 'Bracket that' and 'Quote that' to surround selected text with brackets or quotes. However, it does not include a default voice command to enclose text with vertical bars (|text|).

This **Step-by-Step** command allows you to do so by dictating the command phrase "enclose within vertical bars" when text is selected.

MyCommand Name: enclose within vertical bars

Description: Places vertical bars around the selected text

Group: Dragon – Global Step-by-Step commands

Availability: Global

Command Type: Step-by-Step

Steps:

```
Keystrokes Press Ctrl + C
Type Text Type "|"
Keystrokes Press Ctrl + V
Type Text Type "|"
Keystrokes Press Right
```

Figure 4-3

The MyCommands Editor window, displaying the configuration for the "enclose within vertical bars" command and its required steps.

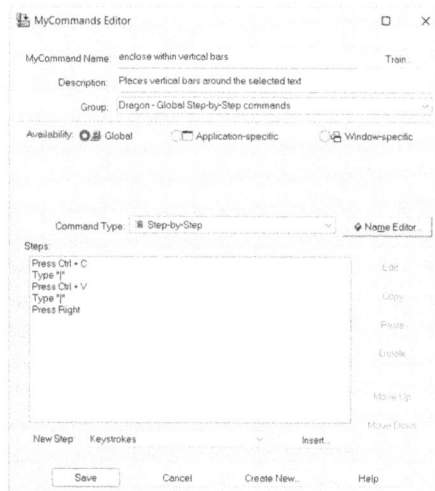

Open a document, select some text, and try it by saying:
"enclose within vertical bars"

Discuss

This command consists of several steps. First, a **Keystrokes** step uses the keyboard shortcut **Ctrl+C** to copy the selected text to the clipboard. Next, a **Type Text** step inserts a **Vertical Bar** symbol, followed by another **Keystrokes** step to paste the contents of the clipboard. Then, a **Type Text** step inserts the second **Vertical Bar** symbol. Finally, a **Keystrokes** step presses the **Right Arrow** key to position the cursor outside the vertical bar.

Global Command for Creating HTML Comments

When writing HTML code, there will undoubtedly be times when you need to include comment text. This involves a two-part process: adding the characters <!-- at the beginning of the comment and --> at the end to mark its conclusion.

This **Global Step-by-Step** command can be used to enclose the selected text within the necessary characters to turn it into an HTML comment by dictating the command phrase "make this a HTML comment". As a global command, it will work in popular text editor applications.

MyCommand Name: make this a HTML comment

Description: Converts the text into a HTML comment

Group: Dragon – Global Step-by-Step commands

Availability: Global

Command Type: Step-by-Step

Steps:

```
Keystrokes Press Ctrl + C
Type Text Type "<!-- "
Keystrokes Press Ctrl + V
Type Text Type " -->"
Keystrokes Press Right
```

Figure 4-4

The MyCommands Editor window, displaying the configuration for the "make this a HTML comment" command and its required steps.

Open a document, select some text, and try it by saying:
"make this a HTML comment"

Discuss

This command consists of several steps. First, a **Keystrokes** step uses the keyboard shortcut **Ctrl+C** to copy the selected text to the clipboard. Next, a **Type Text** step inserts the characters (`<!--`), with a space included after the hyphen. This is followed by another **Keystrokes** step to paste the contents of the clipboard. Then, a **Type Text** step inserts the characters (`.-->`), with a space included before the hyphen. Finally, a **Keystrokes** step presses the **Right Arrow** key to position the cursor outside the characters.

> When deciding on a command phrase that includes an abbreviation, it is best practice to write the abbreviation in capital letters.

Opening the File Explorer Window at a Specific Folder

A user who practices good file management techniques will often create many directories containing numerous subfolders.

While this is a good practice, navigating to a specific file within a folder often involves clicking through multiple levels in Windows File Explorer. Additionally, the user must rely on memory to recall where specific files are located.

Creating a **Step-by-Step** command can speed up this process by opening Windows File Explorer directly to a specific folder. This **Step-by-Step** command opens a folder called 'Accounts Folder' in File Explorer when you dictate the command phrase "open my accounts folder".

MyCommand Name: open my accounts folder

Description: Opens the File Explorer at a specific folder

Group: Dragon – Global Step-by-Step commands

Availability: Global

Command Type: Step-by-Step

Steps:

```
Open (application)
        Target: Explorer
        Arguments: C:\Users\Mike\Desktop\Accounts Folder
        Start in:
        Run: Normal
```

Figure 4-5

The MyCommands Editor window, displaying the configuration for the "open my accounts folder" command and its required steps.

Try it by saying:
"open my accounts folder"

Discuss

This command uses the **Open (application)** step to launch the File Explorer window. The breakdown is as follows: the **Target** field is populated with the word "Explorer", the **Arguments** field contains the full path to the required folder, and the **Run** field is set to "Normal" so that the File Explorer window opens at the same size as it was previously.

The method to create this command varies depending on your version of Dragon. Specifically, in the case of Dragon Professional v16, it also depends on how Dragon was installed and whether you have administrative rights.

If the **Target** field is not available, you will need to click the Browse button to locate the Explorer.exe file. This file is typically found in the following directory: C:\Windows\Explorer.exe

Before running the command, update the Arguments field in the Open (application) step to reflect the destination folder path and folder name on your PC (e.g., C:\Path_to...\FolderName\).

Opening a Specific Document (List command)

Scenario

In your role, you frequently fill out a form for new clients your workplace interacts with. Each time, you find yourself opening the same blank client template document. This repetitive task requires navigating through folders to locate the file, which can be time-consuming.

To streamline your workflow, you want a Dragon voice command that allows you to open the client template document instantly. By dictating a simple command, the document will open, ready for you to input the client's details, eliminating the need to search for it manually each time.

This **Step-by-Step List** command allows you to open a specific Word document stored in a folder by dictating any of the following command phrases: "open client template", "open new client form" or "open client template".

MyCommand Name: <open client template form>

Name of List(s) used: <open client template form>

List items:
open client template form
open new client form
open client template

Description: Opens a specific document.

Group: Dragon – Global Step-by-Step commands

Availability: Global

Command Type: Step-by-Step

Steps:

```
Open (application)
      Target: C:\Users\Mike\Desktop\Clients Folder\New-Client-Template.docx
      Arguments:
      Start in:
      Run: Maximized
```

Figure 4-6

The MyCommands Editor window, displaying the configuration for the "<open client template form>" command and its required steps.

Try it by saying:
"open client template form"

Discuss

This command uses the **Open (application)** step to open the required document. The breakdown is as follows: the **Target** field is populated with the full path and filename, including the file extension. The **Arguments** field is left blank, and the **Run** field is set to "Maximized" so the document opens in a maximized state.

> In this example, an MS Word document is used, assuming that MS Word is installed on your PC. Dragon will execute this command as seamlessly as it would for MS Excel or MS PowerPoint documents. The application that opens depends on the program associated with the document's file type.

The method to create this command varies depending on your version of Dragon. Specifically, in the case of Dragon Professional v16, it also depends on how Dragon was installed and whether you have administrative rights.

If the **Target** field is not available, you will need to click the Browse button to open the Choose Application or Document window, navigate to the required document, select it and click the Open button.

To facilitate dictation of natural language variations for opening the document, we have created a Dragon List command. The List named <open client template form> contains all the voice command phrases that can be dictated to execute the command. You can add alternative command phrases to execute the command by editing the List.

Alternative

This Step-by-Step command can open any type of document. As long as the file extension is included in the filename, Windows will use the associated application to open the document.

> When searching for your document via the Open (application) step Browse button, you will notice that by default, Dragon is set to search for Applications (see Figure 4-7). You will need to change this to All files (*.*) in order that your documents appear in the search.

Figure 4-7

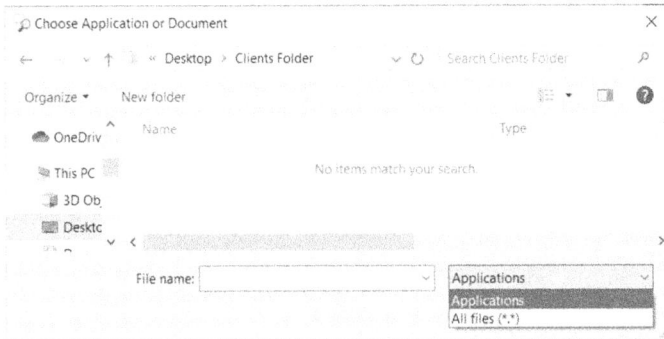

Figure 4-7 shows the Choose Application or Document Window with the File name drop down menu showing the options of whether to show Applications or All files (*.*).

Opening a Specific Document with a Non-Associated Application

This command builds on the previous example. In this scenario, a **Step-by-Step** command is created to open a specific CSV file, not with its default associated application—typically Microsoft Excel—but instead with the Notepad application.

MyCommand Name: open the data file

Description: Opens a specific document with a non-associated application

Group: Dragon – Global Step-by-Step commands

Availability: Global

Command Type: Step-by-Step

Steps:

```
Open (application)
        Target: notepad
        Arguments: C:\Users\Mike\Desktop\Clients Folder\datafile.csv
        Start in:
        Run: Maximized
```

Figure 4-8

The MyCommands Editor window, displaying the configuration for the "open the data file" command and its required steps.

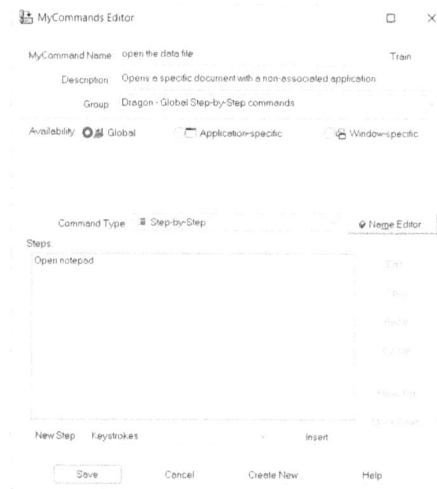

Try it by saying:
"open the data file"

Discuss

This command uses the **Open (application)** step to launch the Notepad application and open the required CSV document. The breakdown is as follows: the **Target** field is populated with the word notepad, and the **Arguments** field contains the full path and filename, including the CSV file extension. The **Run** field is set to "Maximized" to ensure the document opens in a maximized state.

The process for creating this command may vary depending on your version of Dragon. For instance, in Dragon Professional v16, it also depends on how Dragon was installed and whether you have administrative rights.

If the **Target** field is not available, you will need to click the Browse button to open the Choose Application or Document window. From there, navigate to the Notepad executable file, select it and click the Open button.

The Notepad executable file can typically be found in the following location: C:\Windows\System32\notepad.exe.

Opening a Specific Web Page URL in the Default Web Browser (List command)

If you frequently visit specific web pages, you can create a **Step-by-Step** command to open them using voice commands. This **Step-by-Step List** command opens your default browser to a specific website URL when you dictate any of the following command phrases: "open Dragon Professional tutorials" or "dragon tutorials".

MyCommand Name: <open dragon professional tutorials>

Name of List(s) used: <open dragon professional tutorials>

List items:
open Dragon Professional tutorials
dragon tutorials

Description: Opens the default browser at a specific website

Group: Dragon – Global Step-by-Step commands

Availability: Global

Command Type: Step-by-Step

Steps:

```
Open (application)
      Target: https://www.dragonspeechacademy.com/courses/dragon-professional-
learning-hub
      Arguments:
      Start in:
      Run: Maximized
```

Figure 4-9

The MyCommands Editor window, displaying the configuration for the "<open dragon professional tutorials>" command and its required steps.

Try it by saying:
"dragon tutorials"

Discuss

This command uses the **Open (application)** step to open the specified web page. The breakdown is as follows: the **Target** field is populated with the full website URL. The **Arguments** field is left blank, and the **Run** field is set to "Maximized" so the browser opens in a maximized state.

The method to create this command varies depending on your version of Dragon. Specifically, in the case of Dragon Professional v16, it also depends on how Dragon was installed and whether you have administrative rights.

If the **Target** field is not available, click the Browse button to open the Choose Application or Document window. From there, navigate to the executable file of your default browser. For Microsoft Edge, this file is typically located in the following directory: C:\Program Files (x86)\Microsoft\Edge\Application\msedge.exe. After selecting the executable, you will need to populate the **Arguments** field with the full website URL.

To facilitate dictation of natural language variations for opening the web page, we have created a Dragon List command. The List named <open dragon professional tutorials> contains all the voice command phrases that can be dictated to execute the command. You can add alternative command phrases to execute the command by editing the List.

> Browser executable files can typically be found in the following locations:
> Google Chrome: C:\Program Files\Google\Chrome\Application\chrome.exe.
> Firefox: C:\Program Files\Mozilla Firefox\firefox.exe
> MS Edge: C:\Program Files (x86)\Microsoft\Edge\Application\msedge.exe.

Opening a Specific Web Page URL in a Specific Web Browser

This Step-by-Step command builds on the previous one. Instead of opening the default browser, it ensures the web URL opens specifically in Google Chrome when you dictate the command phrase "open the dragon learning hub".

MyCommand Name: open the dragon learning hub

Description: Opens a specific browser at a specific website

Group: Dragon – Global Step-by-Step commands

Availability: Global

Command Type: Step-by-Step

Steps:

```
Open (application)
      Target: Firefox
      Arguments: https://www.dragonspeechacademy.com/courses/dragon-professional-
learning-hub
      Start in:
      Run: Maximized
```

Figure 4-10

The MyCommands Editor window, displaying the configuration for the "open the dragon learning hub" command and its required steps.

Try it by saying:

"open the dragon learning hub"

Discuss

This command uses the **Open (application)** step to open the specified web page in the Firefox browser. The breakdown is as follows: the **Target** field is populated with the word "Firefox", the **Arguments** field is populated with the full website URL, and the **Run** field is set to "Maximized" so the browser opens in a maximized state.

The method to create this command varies depending on your version of Dragon. Specifically, in the case of Dragon Professional v16, it also depends on how Dragon was installed and whether you have administrative rights.

If the **Target** field is not available, click the Browse button to open the Choose Application or Document window. From there, navigate to the executable file of your default browser. For Google Chrome, the executable is typically located in: C:\Program Files (x86)\Google\Chrome\Application\chrome.exe. After selecting the appropriate executable, you will need to populate the **Arguments** field with the full website URL.

Browser executable files can typically be found in the following locations:
Google Chrome: C:\Program Files\Google\Chrome\Application\chrome.exe.
Firefox: C:\Program Files\Mozilla Firefox\firefox.exe
MS Edge: C:\Program Files (x86)\Microsoft\Edge\Application\msedge.exe.

Opening Applications Unknown to Dragon

By default, Dragon recognises many applications, allowing you to use voice commands like 'Open PowerPoint,' 'Open Paint,' 'Open WordPad,' or 'Open Command Prompt' to launch them.

However, for some applications, if we wish to open them by voice, we first need to know the location of the executable file and then we can create a **Step-by-Step** command to open it.

This **Global Step-by-Step** command opens the Notepad++ application when you dictate the command phrase "open notepad plus plus".

MyCommand Name: open notepad plus plus

Description: Opens the Notepad++ application

Group: Dragon – Global Step-by-Step commands

Availability: Global

Command Type: Step-by-Step

Steps:

```
Open (application)
        Target: C:\Program Files (x86)\Notepad++\notepad++.exe
        Arguments:
        Start in:
        Run: Maximized
```

Figure 4-11

The MyCommands Editor window, displaying the configuration for the "open notepad plus plus" command and its required steps.

Try it by saying:

"open notepad plus plus"

Discuss

This **Global Step-by-Step** command uses the **Open (application)** step to open the Notepad++ application. The breakdown is as follows: the **Target** field is populated with the full path and executable filename, including the file extension. The **Arguments** field is left blank, and the **Run** field is set to 'Maximized' so that the Notepad++ application opens in a maximized state.

The method to create this command varies depending on your version of Dragon. Specifically, in the case of Dragon Professional v16, it also depends on how Dragon was installed and whether you have administrative rights.

If the **Target** field is not available, click the Browse button to open the Choose Application or Document window. From there, navigate to the executable file of Notepad++, select the executable, and click the Open button. The executable is typically located in: C:\Program Files (x86)\Notepad++\notepad++.exe.

When deciding on a command phrase that includes punctuation or symbols, it is best practice to write them in word form rather than using the symbols.

Automating a website Login with a Voice Command

Scenario

You frequently log in to your Wikipedia account, but since you prefer not to save your username and password on a shared computer for security reasons, manually entering your credentials every time can be a hassle. To simplify this process, you want to create a voice command that automatically logs you into Wikipedia when you dictate the command phrase "log me into wiki"

This Step-by-Step command will save you time and effort, allowing you to access your account without needing to manually type in your login information each time.

MyCommand Name: log me into wiki

Description: Logs me into Wikipedia

Group: Dragon – Global Step-by-Step commands

Availability: Global

Command Type: Step-by-Step

Steps:

```
Open (application)
        Target:
https://en.wikipedia.org/w/index.php?title=Special:UserLogin&returnto=Main+Page
        Arguments:
        Start in:
        Run: Maximized
Wait 50 milliseconds
Keystrokes Press Ctrl + C
Type Text Type "MrMike23"
Keystrokes Press Tab
Type Text Type "12345ABCDE"
Keystrokes Press Enter
```

Figure 4-12

The MyCommands Editor window, displaying the
configuration for the "log me into wiki" command and its
required steps.

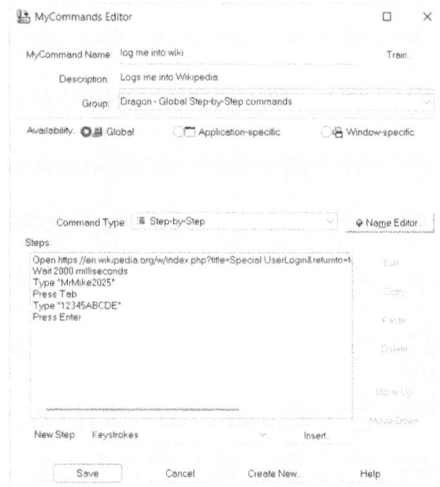

Try it by saying:

"log me into wiki"

Discuss

This command consists of several steps. First, an **Open (application)** step opens the browser at the Wikipedia login page.

Next, a **Wait** step ensures the webpage has fully loaded and the cursor is positioned in the Username field. A **Type Text** step then inputs the username, followed by a **Keystrokes** step that emulates pressing the **Tab** key to move to the Password field. Another **Type Text** step inputs the password. Finally, a **Keystrokes** step presses the **Enter** key to complete the login process.

The method to create this command varies depending on your version of Dragon. Specifically, in the case of Dragon Professional v16, it also depends on how Dragon was installed and whether you have administrative rights.

When creating the **Open (application)** step, if the **Target** field is not available, click the Browse button to open the Choose Application or Document window. From there, navigate to the executable file of your default browser. For Microsoft Edge, this file is typically located in the following directory: C:\Program Files (x86)\Microsoft\Edge\Application\msedge.exe. After selecting the executable, you will need to populate the **Arguments** field with the full website URL.

> You may need to adjust the Wait time to accommodate your computer's processing speed and internet speed to ensure the command works successfully.

Opening Websites and Turning Off the Microphone with a Single Voice Command

Scenario

Imagine starting your day by quickly accessing the three websites you rely on most, including your favourite radio station. Instead of manually opening each site, you want to streamline this process with a single voice command. To ensure minimal distractions, you also want Dragon to first turn off the microphone before opening the websites.

This Step-by-Step command enables you to say, "open my favourite websites" prompting Dragon to turn off the microphone and then open all three sites for you.

MyCommand Name: open my favourite websites

Description: Turns the microphone off and opens three websites

Group: Dragon – Global Step-by-Step commands

Availability: Global

Command Type: Step-by-Step

Steps:

```
Microphone Offt Microphone Off
Open (application)
        Target: www.bbcworldservice.com
        Arguments:
        Start in:
        Run: Maximized
Open (application)
        Target: https://dragonspeechtips.com/
        Arguments:
        Start in:
Run: Maximized
Open (application)
        Target: https://www.dragonspeechacademy.com/courses/dragon-professional-
learning-hub
        Arguments:
        Start in:
Run: Maximized
```

Figure 4-13

The MyCommands Editor window, displaying the configuration for the "open my favourite websites" command and its required steps.

Try it by saying:
"open my favourite websites"

Discuss

This command consists of several steps. First, a **Microphone Off** step turns off the Dragon microphone.

Next, three **Open (application)** steps launch the browser and open three tabs for the specified URLs.

The method to create this command varies depending on your version of Dragon. Specifically, in the case of Dragon Professional v16, it also depends on how Dragon was installed and whether you have administrative rights.

When creating an **Open (application)** step, if the **Target** field is not available, click the Browse button to open the Choose Application or Document window. From there, navigate to the executable file of your default browser. For Microsoft Edge, this file is typically located in the following directory: C:\Program Files (x86)\Microsoft\Edge\Application\msedge.exe. After selecting the executable, you will need to populate the **Arguments** field with the full website URL.

> Browser executable files can typically be found in the following locations:
> Google Chrome: C:\Program Files\Google\Chrome\Application\chrome.exe.
> Firefox: C:\Program Files\Mozilla Firefox\firefox.exe.

Creating a New Google Docs with a Voice Command

Scenario

From time to time, you need to create a new Google Docs document quickly. However, manually switching to your browser, navigating to the correct URL, and clicking through the required steps can be time-consuming and interrupt your workflow.

To streamline this process, you can use a **Global Step-by-Step** command. By simply dictating the command phrase "open new google doc" from any environment, Dragon will open your default browser, navigate to Google Docs, and create a new document—ready for you to start working immediately. This saves time and eliminates the need for repetitive mouse and keyboard actions.

MyCommand Name: open new google doc

Description: Switches to the browser and opens a new Google Docs

Group: Dragon – Global Step-by-Step commands

Availability: Global

Command Type: Step-by-Step

Steps:

```
Open (application)
        Target: https://doc.new
        Arguments:
        Start in:
        Run: Maximized
```

Figure 4-14

The MyCommands Editor window, displaying the configuration for the "open new google doc" command and its required steps.

Try it by saying:
"open new google doc"

Discuss

This command uses the **Open (application)** step to launch the default browser and open a new Google Doc. The breakdown is as follows: the Target field is populated with the URL `https://doc.new`. The **Arguments** field remains blank, and the **Run** field is set to "Maximized" to ensure the browser opens in full-screen mode.

The method to create this command varies depending on your version of Dragon. Specifically, in the case of Dragon Professional v16, it also depends on how Dragon was installed and whether you have administrative rights.

If the **Target** field is not available, click the Browse button to open the Choose Application or Document window. From there, navigate to the executable file of your default browser. For Google Chrome, this file is typically located in the following directory: C:\Program Files (x86)\Google\Chrome\Application\chrome.exe. After selecting the executable, you will need to populate the **Arguments** field with the URL `https://doc.new`.

For this command to work seamlessly, ensure you are already logged into your Google account.

Browser executable files can typically be found in the following locations:
Google Chrome: C:\Program Files\Google\Chrome\Application\chrome.exe.
Firefox: C:\Program Files\Mozilla Firefox\firefox.exe
MS Edge: C:\Program Files (x86)\Microsoft\Edge\Application\msedge.exe.

Alternative

To create alternative **Step-by-Step** commands for a new Google Sheet or Google Slide, replace the URL `https://doc.new` with `https://sheet.new` for Google Sheets or `https://slide.new` for Google Slides.

Adding a Comment to a Google Doc

Whilst working within your Google Docs, you may want to add a comment to the document.

This Global Step-by-Step command opens the comment window in the active Google Doc when you dictate the command phrase "insert a comment"

MyCommand Name: insert a comment

Description: Inserts a comment into a Google Doc

Group: Dragon – Global Step-by-Step commands

Availability: Global

Command Type: Step-by-Step

Steps:

Keystrokes Press Ctrl + Alt + M

Figure 4-15

The MyCommands Editor window, displaying the configuration for the "insert a comment" command and its required steps.

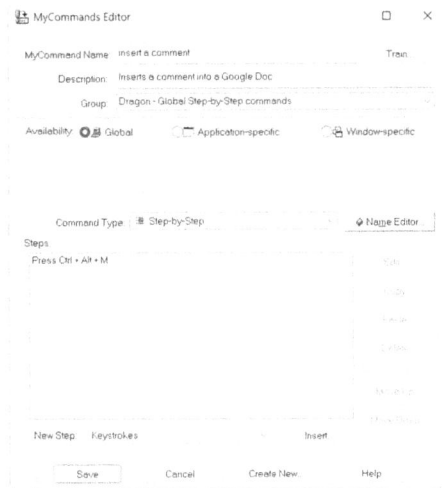

Ensure Google Docs is the active window, select some text, and try it by saying:
"insert a comment"

Discuss

This command uses a **Keystrokes** step to perform the keyboard shortcut **Ctrl+Alt+M**

Insert a Horizontal Line within a Google Doc

In Google Docs, you may want to add a horizontal line to separate sections of your text.

This **Step-by-Step** command inserts a horizontal line at the cursor's position in the document when you dictate the command phrase, "insert horizontal line".

MyCommand Name: insert horizontal line

Description: Inserts a horizontal line into a Google Doc

Group: Dragon – Global Step-by-Step commands

Availability: Global

Command Type: Step-by-Step

Steps:

```
Keystrokes Press Shift + Alt + I
Send Keys Send Keys "R"
```

Figure 4-16

The MyCommands Editor window, displaying the configuration for the "insert horizontal line" command and its required steps.

Ensure Google Docs is the active window, position the cursor, and try it by saying:
"insert horizontal line"

Discuss

This command starts with a Keystrokes step using **Shift+Alt+I** to open the Google Docs Insert menu, ensuring the command works regardless of the active menu. The shortcut also reveals the Key Tips, showing available shortcuts like the underlined **R** in the Horizontal line option. Next, a **Send Keys** step presses **R** to select it.

Creating Checkboxes for Selected Lines in Google Docs

Scenario

Imagine you've completed a detailed To-Do list in Google Docs and want to make it more interactive by adding checkboxes beside each item. Since Google Docs does not offer a dedicated keyboard shortcut for inserting checkboxes, manually adding them can be time-consuming.

To streamline this process, you can create a Step-by-Step command that automates the necessary actions.

This Step-by-Step command creates checkboxes for the selected lines when you dictate the command phrase, "create checkboxes".

MyCommand Name: create checkboxes

Description: creates checkboxes for the selected lines

Group: Dragon – Global Step-by-Step commands

Availability: Global

Command Type: Step-by-Step

Steps:

```
Keystrokes Press Shift + Alt + O
Send Keys Send Keys "T"
Send Keys Send Keys "B"
Send Keys Send Keys "{Right 2}"
Keystrokes Press Enter
```

Figure 4-17

The MyCommands Editor window, displaying the configuration for the "create checkboxes" command and its required steps.

Ensure Google Docs is the active window, select some lines, and try it by saying:
"create checkboxes"

Discuss

This command begins with a Keystrokes step to execute the keyboard shortcut **Shift+Alt+O**, switching to the Google Docs Format menu and ensuring the command works regardless of the currently active menu. This shortcut also reveals the Key Tips for the Format menu, where Google Docs provides visual clues to available keyboard shortcuts, such as the line underneath the letter **T** in the Bullets and numbering option.

A **Send Keys** step presses the letter **T** to select the Bullets and numbering option, followed by another **Send Keys** step to press the letter **B,** to reveal the Bulleted list menu. To select the Checkboxes option, we need to press the Right Arrow key twice. This is achieved using a **Send Keys** step, where the command {Right 2} is inserted into the **Send Keys** step window.

Finally, a **Keystrokes** step is used to press the **Enter** key.

For this command to work, the selected text must not already have bullets applied.

Saving a Google Doc as a Microsoft Word Document

Occasionally, you may want to distribute your Google Docs as Microsoft Word documents.

This **Step-by-Step** command saves a Microsoft Word version of the active Google Doc to your Downloads folder.

MyCommand Name: download as a word document

Description: download the active Google Doc as a Word document

Group: Dragon – Global Step-by-Step commands

Availability: Global

Command Type: Step-by-Step

Steps:

```
Keystrokes Press Shift + Alt + F
Send Keys Send Keys "D"
Send Keys Send Keys "X"
```

Figure 4-18

The MyCommands Editor window, displaying the configuration for the "download as a word document" command and its required steps.

Ensure Google Docs is the active window, select some lines, and try it by saying:
"download as a word document"

Discuss

This command begins with a **Keystrokes** step to execute the keyboard shortcut **Shift+Alt+F**, opening the Google Docs File menu and ensuring the command functions regardless of the currently active menu.

Two **Send Keys** steps are then used to press the letter **D**, followed by the letter **X**.

Vertically Aligning and Centering the Content of the Selected Cells(s) in Google Sheets

Scenario

As part of your workflow, you often vertically align and center the contents of the cells within your Google Sheets. This involves a fair amount of keyboard shortcuts or mouse movement to achieve this, and you require a voice command that executes the task when you dictate the command phrase "align center and vertical".

This **Step-by-Step** command carries out the task.

MyCommand Name: align center and vertical

Description: aligns the selected Google sheets cell content center and vertical

Group: Dragon – Global Step-by-Step commands

Availability: Global

Command Type: Step-by-Step

Steps:

```
Keystrokes Press Ctrl + Shift + E
Keystrokes Press Shift + Alt + O
Send Keys Send Keys "A"
Send Keys Send Keys "M"
```

Figure 4-19

The MyCommands Editor window, displaying the configuration for the "align center and vertical" command and its required steps.

Ensure Google Sheets is the active window, select a cell(s), and try it by saying:

"align center and vertical"

Discuss

This command begins with a **Keystrokes** step to execute the keyboard shortcut **Ctrl+Shift+E**, to center the cell(s) content. Next, another Keystrokes step performs the keyboard shortcut **Shift+Alt+O**, opening the Google Docs Format menu and ensuring the command functions regardless of the currently active menu.

Two **Send Keys** steps are then used to press the letter **A**, followed by the letter **M**, to align the content vertically.

Saving a Google Sheet as a Comma-Separated Values (CSV) File

Occasionally, you may want to distribute your Google Sheets as Comma-separated values (CSV) files.

This **Step-by-Step** command saves a CSV file version of the active Google Sheet to your Downloads folder.

MyCommand Name: download as a CSV file

Description: download the active Google Sheet as a CSV document

Group: Dragon – Global Step-by-Step commands

Availability: Global

Command Type: Step-by-Step

Steps:

```
Keystrokes Press Shift + Alt + F
Send Keys Send Keys "D"
Send Keys Send Keys "C"
```

Figure 4-20

The MyCommands Editor window, displaying the configuration for the "download as a CSV" command and its required steps.

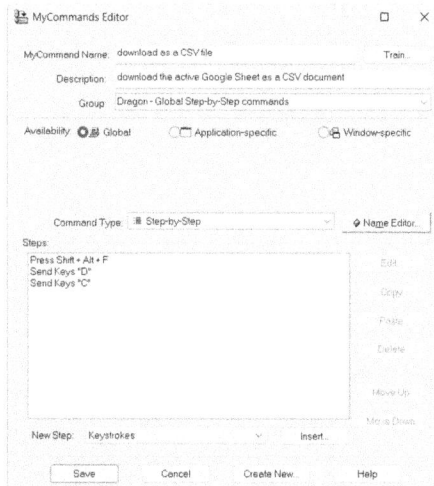

Ensure Google Docs is the active window, and try it by saying:
"download as a CSV file"

Discuss

This command begins with a **Keystrokes** step to execute the keyboard shortcut **Shift+Alt+F**, opening the Google Docs File menu and ensuring the command functions regardless of the currently active menu.

Two **Send Keys** steps are then used to press the letter **D**, followed by the letter **C**.

> When deciding on a command phrase that includes an abbreviation, it is best practice to write the abbreviation in capital letters.

Section 5: Dragon Commands for Microsoft Word

Dragon Commands for Microsoft Word

Dragon, by default, includes numerous commands that perform MS Word functions. Typical commands include the ability to set font colours, insert page breaks, and apply header styles. In addition, Dragon provides more complex commands such as marking text and enabling the creation of indexes.

This section introduces several useful commands not provided by Dragon out of the box. These custom-created commands are designed to enhance productivity when using Microsoft Word and have been thoroughly tested with **MS Word Office 365**.

They are also compatible with earlier versions of MS Word.

In This Part: Step-by-Step Commands
21–30

Closing a Word Document Without Being Prompted to Save Changes

Scenario

You often work on Word documents where saving changes is unnecessary and closing them without prompts would save time. Instead of navigating menus or responding to save prompts, you want a voice command to simplify the process. By saying "close without saving", Dragon immediately closes the active Word document without prompting to save, streamlining the task into a single command.

This Step-by-Step command efficiently combines actions, eliminating the need for multiple voice commands.

MyCommand Name: close without saving

Description: Closes the active document without prompting to save

Group: Dragon – Microsoft Word Step-by-Step commands

Availability: Application-specific

Application: Microsoft Word

Command Type: Step-by-Step

Steps:

```
Keystrokes Press Ctrl + W
Keystrokes Press Alt + N
```

Figure 5-0

The MyCommands Editor window, displaying the configuration for the "close without saving" command and its required steps.

Ensure MS Word is the active window, the correct document is open, and then say:

"close without saving"

Discuss

Two steps are required for this command. First, a **Keystrokes** step performs the keyboard shortcut **Ctrl+W** to close MS Word. Then, another **Keystrokes** step performs the keyboard shortcut **Alt+N**, which emulates clicking the Don't Save button.

Deleting All Content in a Document with a Single Voice Command

By default, Dragon does not provide a voice command to delete all text and objects within a document in one step. To achieve this, you would first dictate the command phrase "select all", wait for the content to be selected, and then dictate the command "Delete That".

This **Step-by-Step** command eliminates the need to dictate two separate voice commands, allowing you to complete the process simply by dictating the command phrase "delete everything".

MyCommand Name: delete everything

Description: Deletes all the content of the active document

Group: Dragon – Microsoft Word Step-by-Step commands

Availability: Application-specific

Application: Microsoft Word

Command Type: Step-by-Step

Steps:

```
Keystrokes Press Ctrl + A
Keystrokes Press Delete
```

Figure 5-1

The MyCommands Editor window, displaying the configuration for the "delete everything" command and its required steps.

Make sure MS Word is the active window and try it by saying:
"delete everything"

Discuss

This Step-by-Step command utilises the keyboard shorts **Ctrl+A** and the pressing of the delete key to perform the action. Therefore, a **Keystrokes** step is used to perform the **Ctrl+A,** and a **Keystrokes** step is used to carry out the deletion.

Alternative

This command can be easily adjusted for use in other applications. Changing the **Availability** option to '**Global**' will make this command accessible across all applications.

It is important to understand the impact of pressing Ctrl+A in specific applications. For example, in PowerPoint, selecting an object on a slide and then pressing Ctrl+A selects all the objects on the active slide only. However, selecting a slide thumbnail and pressing Ctrl+A selects all slides.

Changing the Document Background Colour to Sepia

Scenario

You share a computer in the workplace, and colour blindness is a concern. You need a quick way to change the background colour of an MS Word document to your preferred colour, sepia, to enhance readability.

This **Step-by-Step** command allows you to use the voice command phrase "switch to sepia" to change the document to Read Mode with the background set to sepia.

MyCommand Name: switch to sepia

Description: Changes the background colour of the active word document to Sepia

Group: Dragon – Microsoft Word Step-by-Step commands

Availability: Application-specific

Application: Microsoft Word

Command Type: Step-by-Step

Steps:

```
Keystrokes Press Alt + W
Send Keys Send Keys "F"
Wait Wait 50 milliseconds
Keystrokes Press Alt + W
Send Keys Send Keys "G"
Send Keys Send Keys "S"
```

Figure 5-2

The MyCommands Editor window, displaying the configuration for the "switch to sepia" command and its required steps.

Make sure MS Word is the active window and try it by saying:
"switch to sepia"

Discuss

This command consists of several steps. First, a **Keystrokes** step uses the keyboard shortcut **Alt+W** to switch to the MS Word View menu, ensuring the command works regardless of the currently active Word menu. A **Send Keys** step then presses the letter **F** to select Read Mode.

Next, a **Wait** step introduces a brief delay to allow MS Word time to switch to Read Mode.

Finally, another **Keystrokes** step performs the **Alt+W** keyboard shortcut again, followed by two **Send Keys** steps to press the keys **G** and **S**, selecting the Sepia option.

> You may need to adjust the Wait time to accommodate your computer's processing speed to ensure the command works successfully.

Displaying Line Numbers in Documents

Scenario

Occasionally, you may need to make reference (perhaps over the telephone) to a specific line within a document. You might describe it as: Page 3; paragraph 4; 3 lines up. This can be tedious. However, MS Word offers a solution, by allowing line numbers to appear, making editing or clarification much easier.

This **Step-by-Step** command enables you to use the voice command phrase "show the line numbers" to display line numbers within a document.

MyCommand Name: show the line numbers

Description: Shows the line numbers in a MS Word document

Group: Dragon – Microsoft Word Step-by-Step commands

Availability: Application-specific

Application: Microsoft Word

Command Type: Step-by-Step

Steps:

```
Keystrokes Press Alt + P
Send Keys Send Keys "L"
Send Keys Send Keys "N"
Send Keys Send Keys "C"
```

Figure 5-3

The MyCommands Editor window, displaying the configuration for the "show the line numbers" command and its required steps.

Make sure MS Word is the active window and try it by saying:

"show the line numbers"

Discuss

This command consists of several steps. First, a **Keystrokes** step uses the keyboard shortcut **Alt+P** to switch to the MS Word Layout menu, ensuring the command functions regardless of the currently active menu. Next, three **Send Keys** steps press the letters **F**, **N**, and **C** in sequence to reveal the line numbers.

> The line numbers when shown are for display purposes only and form no part of the actual document.

Inserting a Simple Text Box within a Word Document

Scenario

You frequently use Text Boxes in Word to highlight key points, but manually navigating through Word's menus to insert a simple Text Box can be repetitive and time-consuming, especially when you're working on multiple documents or tight deadlines.

Figure 5-4

Figure 5-4 shows a Simple Text Box inserted within a Word document.

You'd like a voice command, that when you say, "insert simple text box", allows Dragon to automatically navigate the menus and insert a simple Text Box into your document.

This **Step-by-Step** command performs this task, saving you time and streamlining your workflow.

MyCommand Name: insert simple text box

Description: Inserts a Simple Text Box into a MS Word document

Group: Dragon – Microsoft Word Step-by-Step commands

Availability: Application-specific

Application: Microsoft Word

Command Type: Step-by-Step

Steps:

```
Keystrokes Press Alt + N
Send Keys Send Keys "X"
Keystrokes Press Enter
```

Figure 5-5

The MyCommands Editor window, displaying the configuration for the "insert simple text box" command and its required steps.

Make sure MS Word is the active window, place your cursor in the text, and try it by saying:

"insert simple text box"

Discuss

Three steps are required for this command. First, a **Keystrokes** step performs the keyboard shortcut **Alt+N** to open the Insert menu. Next, a **Send Keys** step presses the letter **X** to select the Simple Text Box option. Finally, a **Keystrokes** step presses the **Enter** key to confirm the selection.

Applying a Specific Highlight Colour to the Selected Text

Scenario

As part of your workflow, you often need to highlight text in a specific colour. Normally, this involves extensive mouse movements or multiple voice commands.

To streamline the process, you want to use a single voice command. By simply selecting the text and dictating the phrase "highlight in turquoise", Dragon will automatically apply the predefined highlight colour, saving time and reducing repetitive actions.

This **Step-by-Step** command highlights the selected text with the colour turquoise.

MyCommand Name: highlight in turquoise

Description: Highlights the selected text in turquoise

Group: Dragon – Microsoft Word Step-by-Step commands

Availability: Application-specific

Application: Microsoft Word

Command Type: Step-by-Step

Steps:

```
Keystrokes Press Alt + H
Keystrokes Press Alt + I
Send Keys Send Keys "{Right 3}"
Keystrokes Press Enter
```

Figure 5-6

The MyCommands Editor window, displaying the configuration for the "highlight in turquoise" command and its required steps.

Make sure MS Word is the active window, select the required text, and try it by saying:
"highlight in turquoise"

Discuss

This command consists of several steps. First, a **Keystrokes** step uses the keyboard shortcut **Alt+H** to switch to the MS Word Home menu, ensuring the command works regardless of the currently active Word menu. Another **Keystrokes** step is used to emulate pressing the keyboard shortcut **Alt+I**, which selects the highlights colour palette.

Next, a **Send Keys** steps emulates pressing the **Right Arrow** key three times to navigate to the turquoise colour. Finally, a **Keystrokes** step presses the **Enter** key to confirm the highlight colour and finish the process.

When inserting the text within the "Send Keys" step, it is important to include a space after the code and before the value such as in {Right 3}.

Applying a Specific Highlight Colour and Text Colour to the Selected Text (List command)

Scenario

This command builds on the previous example. In this scenario, we create a **Step-by-Step List** command that applies the highlight colour yellow and changes the text colour to blue for the selected text.

Since we need a command that responds to the phrases "convert to yellow and blue" or "convert to blue and yellow" a List command is created. This eliminates the need to remember the exact command phrase.

MyCommand Name: <apply_my_highlight_style>

Name of List(s) used: <apply_my_highlight_style>

List items:
convert to yellow and blue
convert to blue and yellow
highlight my way

Description: Changes the text to my highlighted style

Group: Dragon – Microsoft Word Step-by-Step commands

Availability: Application-specific

Application: Microsoft Word

Command Type: Step-by-Step

Steps:

```
Keystrokes Press Alt + H
Send Keys Send Keys "F"
Send Keys Send Keys "C"
Send Keys Send Keys "{Down 5}"
Send Keys Send Keys "{Right 3}"
Keystrokes Press Space
Keystrokes Press Alt + H
Keystrokes Press Alt + I
Keystrokes Press Enter
```

Figure 5-7

The MyCommands Editor window, displaying the configuration for the "<apply_my_highlight_style>" command and its required steps.

Make sure MS Word is the active window, select the required text, and try it by saying:

"convert to yellow and blue", "convert to blue and yellow"

Discuss

This command consists of several steps. First, a **Keystrokes** step executes the keyboard shortcut **Alt+H** to switch to the MS Word Home menu, ensuring the command functions regardless of the currently active Word menu.

Next, two **Send Keys** steps press the letters **F** and **C** to open the text colour options. Then, two additional **Send Keys** steps press the **Down Arrow** key **five** times, followed by the **Right Arrow** key **three** times to select the desired text colour. A **Keystrokes** step presses the **Space Bar** to confirm the chosen colour.

To apply a highlight colour, another **Keystrokes** step uses the **Alt+H** shortcut to return to the MS Word Home menu. A **Keystrokes** step then presses **Alt+I** to open the Highlight colour palette. As the default yellow is preselected, a final **Keystrokes** step presses the **Enter** key to confirm the highlight colour.

To allow for natural language variations when dictating this command, we created a Dragon List command. The List, named <apply_my_highlight_style>, contains all the voice command phrases that can trigger the command. You can edit the List to add alternative phrases for executing the command.

> When inserting the text within the "Send Keys" step, it is important to include a space after the code and before the value such as in {Down 5}.

Applying a Custom Text Style to the Selected Text (List command)

Scenario

As part of your workflow, you frequently need to change the text style of selected text to Small Caps, Font Comic Sans, Size 12, and the colour purple. Normally, this requires extensive mouse movement or multiple voice commands to achieve.

You would like to streamline this process with a single voice command by simply selecting the text and dictating any of the following command phrases: "change to my style", "apply custom style" or "apply my custom style". Dragon will then automatically apply the predefined style to the selected text, reducing the need for repetitive actions and minimising the chance of errors.

This **Step-by-Step List** command changes the text style of the selected text.

MyCommand Name: <apply_custom_style>

Name of List(s) used: <apply_custom_style>

List items:
change to my style
apply custom style
apply my custom style

Description: Changes the text style of the selected text

Group: Dragon – Microsoft Word Step-by-Step commands

Availability: Application-specific

Application: Microsoft Word

Command Type: Step-by-Step

Steps:

```
Keystrokes Press Ctrl + D
Keystrokes Press Alt + N
Keystrokes Press Alt + F
Type Text Type "Comic Sans MS"
Keystrokes Press Alt + S
Type Text Type "12"
Keystrokes Press Alt + M
Keystrokes Press Alt + C
Send Keys Send Keys "{Down 6}"
Send Keys Send Keys "{Right 8}"
Keystrokes Press Enter
Send Keys Send Keys "{Tab 11}"
Keystrokes Press Enter
```

Figure 5-8

The MyCommands Editor window, displaying the configuration for the "<apply_custom_style>" command and its required steps.

Make sure MS Word is the active window, select the required text, and try it by saying:

"change to my style", "apply my custom style"

Discuss

This command consists of several steps. First, a **Keystrokes** step uses the keyboard shortcut **Ctrl+D** to open the Font window. Since the required options are located within the Font tab, we use a **Keystrokes** step to perform the keyboard shortcut **Alt+N** to select the Font tab. Applications like Microsoft Word provide clues to available keyboard shortcuts, as seen with the underlined "**F**" in the Font option, indicating that **Alt+F** can be used to select it. A **Keystrokes** step is used to perform this action.

Next, a **Type Text** step is used to insert the font name "**Comic Sans MS**" (the font name must be written in full as seen in the Font menu). The next two steps involve a **Keystrokes** step followed by a **Type Text** step to select the Size option and populate the value with the number **12**. A **Keystrokes** step is used to perform **Alt+M**, which checks the Small Caps checkbox, followed by a **Keystrokes** step **Alt+C** to select the colour option.

Next, two **Send Keys** steps emulate pressing the **Down** and **Right Arrow** keys to navigate to the required colour. These **Send Keys** steps allow us to specify how many times the keys should be pressed. A **Keystrokes** step is used to press the **Enter** key to confirm the colour, followed by a **Send Keys** step to emulate pressing the **Tab** key **11** times to navigate to the **OK** button. Finally, a **Keystrokes** step presses the **Enter** key to finish the process.

To allow for natural language variations when dictating this command, we created a Dragon List command. The List, named <apply_custom_style>, contains all the voice command phrases that can trigger the command. You can edit the List to add alternative phrases for executing the command.

Applying Custom Character Spacing to the Selected Text

Scenario

As part of your workflow, you often need to adjust the character spacing of text to a specific setting. Instead of manually navigating through the menus each time, you would like a more efficient way to do this. You want a voice command that, when you select some text and dictate the phrase "character spacing zero point five" Dragon automatically changes the character spacing to "Condensed by 0.5," saving you time and effort.

This **Step-by-Step** command performs this task, saving you time and streamlining your workflow.

MyCommand Name: character spacing zero point five

Description: Changes the character spacing of the selected text to Condensed by 0.5

Group: Dragon – Microsoft Word Step-by-Step commands

Availability: Application-specific

Application: Microsoft Word

Command Type: Step-by-Step

Steps:

```
Keystrokes Press Alt + H
Send Keys Send Keys "F"
Send Keys Send Keys "N"
Keystrokes Press Alt + V
Keystrokes Press Alt + S
Send Keys Send Keys "C"
Keystrokes Press Tab
Type Text Type "0.5"
Keystrokes Press Enter
```

Figure 5-9

The MyCommands Editor window, displaying the configuration for the "character spacing zero point five" command and its required steps.

Make sure MS Word is the active window, select the required text, and try it by saying:
"character spacing zero point five"

Discuss

This command consists of several steps. First, a **Keystrokes** step uses the keyboard shortcut **Alt+H** to switch to the MS Word Home menu, ensuring the command works regardless of the currently active menu.

Next, two **Send Keys** steps are used to press the letters **F** and then **N** to open the Font window.

As the options required are located within the Advanced Tab, we use a **Keystrokes** step to perform the keyboard shortcut **Alt+W** to select the Advanced Tab. Microsoft Word offers clues to help identify available keyboard shortcuts, as seen with the underlined "**S**" in the Spacing option, indicating that **Alt+S** can be used to select it. A **Keystrokes** step is used to perform this action.

Next, a **Send Keys** step presses the letter **C** to select Condensed, followed by a **Keystrokes** step to **Tab** to the "**By**" field. A **Type Text** step is then used to insert the value **0.5**. Finally, a **Keystrokes** step presses the **Enter** key to confirm the selection.

☞ When deciding on a command phrase that includes a number. It is best practice to write the number in word form rather than using the numeral.

Applying Custom Paragraph Settings with a Single Voice Command

Scenario

You frequently need to adjust paragraph settings in your documents by setting the hanging value to 1.7, changing the alignment to justified, applying a left indent of 1.1 cm, and enabling the Page Break Before option. While creating a custom style could streamline this process, you prefer to avoid using the mouse or keyboard or having to dictate multiple voice commands.

To save time and eliminate unnecessary mouse and keyboard actions, you want a single voice command. By saying "apply custom paragraph settings" Dragon will instantly apply these specific paragraph adjustments to the selected text, streamlining your workflow and reducing the risk of errors.

This Step-by-Step List command changes the paragraph settings of the selected text.

MyCommand Name: apply custom paragraph settings

Description: Changes the paragraph settings of the selected text

Group: Dragon – Microsoft Word Step-by-Step commands

Availability: Application-specific

Application: Microsoft Word

Command Type: Step-by-Step

Steps:

```
Keystrokes Press Alt + H
Send Keys Send Keys "P"
Send Keys Send Keys "G"
Keystrokes Press Alt + I
Keystrokes Press Alt + G
Send Keys Send Keys "J"
Keystrokes Press Alt + S
Send Keys Send Keys "H"
Keystrokes Press Tab
Type Text Type "1.7"
Keystrokes Press Alt + L
Type Text Type "1.1 cm"
Keystrokes Press Alt + P
Keystrokes Press Alt + B
Keystrokes Press Enter
```

Figure 5-10

The MyCommands Editor window, displaying the configuration for the "apply custom paragraph settings" command and its required steps.

Make sure MS Word is the active window, select the required text, and try it by saying:

"apply custom paragraph settings"

Discuss

This command consists of several steps. First, a **Keystrokes** step uses the keyboard shortcut **Alt+H** to switch to the MS Word Home menu, ensuring the command works regardless of the currently active menu.

Next, two **Send Keys** steps are used to press the letters **P** and then **G** to open the Paragraph window.

As the first set of options required are located within the Indents and Spacings tab, we use a **Keystrokes** step to perform the keyboard shortcut **Alt+I** to select the tab.

As Microsoft Word provides clues to help identify available keyboard shortcuts, such as the underlined "G" in the alignment option, indicating that **Alt+G** can be used to select it. A **Keystrokes** step is used to perform this action, followed by a **Send Keys** step to press the letter **J** to select the Justified alignment option.

The same techniques are used to select the Special option and choose Hanging. A **Keystrokes** step presses the **Tab** key to navigate to the value field, and a **Type Text** step inserts the value **1.7**. Similarly, another **Keystrokes** step followed by a **Type Text** step selects the Indent option and applies a value of **1.1 cm**.

To switch to the Line and Page Breaks tab, a **Keystrokes** step is used to emulate pressing **Alt+P**. Another **Keystrokes** step is then used to press **Alt+B** to enable the Page Break Before option. Finally, a **Keystrokes** step presses the **Enter** key to confirm the settings and complete the process.

Section 6: Dragon Commands for Microsoft Outlook (Classic)

Dragon Commands for Microsoft Outlook (Classic)

The Dragon application - out of the box - works well with the installed application version of Microsoft Outlook represented by the Full Text Control Indicator (small green indicator) in the DragonBar. Typical commands include the ability to easily create and reply to emails using Outlook specific voice commands.

This section provides several useful Dragon Step-by-Step commands that enable you to perform tasks and functions within MS Outlook by voice. These commands have been tested with the **Office 365 Outlook (classic) application**. While the application offers a wide range of shortcut key combinations for various functions, remembering them can be challenging. Instead, you can create Step-by-Step commands to execute popular Outlook functions simply by dictating easy-to-remember voice commands.

In This Part: Step-by-Step Commands

31–37

Write an Email to a Specific Person

Scenario

As part of your job, you frequently write emails to a specific person and want a voice command that, when used within Microsoft Outlook, opens a new email, automatically populates the **To:** field with the person's email address, and places the cursor in the **Subject** field, ready for you to dictate the subject text.

This voice command replaces the individual steps required to carry out such a task when Peter Smith is the intended recipient.

MyCommand Name: email peter smith

Description: Creates a new email to Peter Smith

Group: Dragon – Microsoft Outlook Step-by-Step commands

Availability: Application-specific

Application: Microsoft Outlook

Command Type: Step-by-Step

Steps:

```
Keystrokes Press Ctrl + 1
Keystrokes Press Ctrl + N
Type Text Type "peter.smith@youremail.com"
Keystrokes Press Tab
Send Keys Send Keys "{Tab 2}"
```

Figure 6-0

The MyCommands Editor window, displaying the configuration for the "email peter smith" command and its required steps.

Make sure MS Outlook is the active window and try it by saying:

"email peter smith"

Discuss

This command consists of several steps to automate the process of composing a new email with an intended recipient in MS Outlook. First, a **Keystrokes** step uses the keyboard shortcut **Ctrl+1** to switch to the Mail section of Microsoft Outlook. Next, another **Keystrokes** step performs the keyboard shortcut **Ctrl+N** to create a new email and automatically place the cursor in the **To:** field. Finally, a **Type Text** step is used to enter the desired email address.

To confirm the email address, the **Tab** key is pressed, achieved through a **Keystrokes** step. To move the cursor to the **Subject** field, the **Tab** key needs to be pressed two times. This action is emulated using a **Send Keys** step, where the command {Tab 2} is inserted in the **Send Keys** step window.

> When inserting the text within the "Send Keys" step, it is important to include a space after the code and before the value such as in {Tab 2}.

Alternative

You can create your own version by creating a new copy of the command, editing the command phrase required to execute the command in the **MyCommand Name** field, and edit the recipient's email address by updating the email address entered in the **Type Text** step.

Additionally, if you want to move the cursor directly to the body of the email, you can modify the **Tab** value from 2 to 3 in the **Send Keys** step. This will allow you to begin typing the content of your email without manually clicking in the body area.

Reply to an Email and Setup a Meeting

Scenario

You often need to reply to emails by scheduling meetings, but Dragon doesn't have a built-in voice command for this action. This can be frustrating and time-consuming, especially when you have many emails to respond to and meeting dates to set up.

To streamline this process, this simple voice command allows you to reply to a selected email using Outlook's **Reply with Meeting** function. Once the new window opens, the **Start Date** field is selected, ready for you to insert a date.

MyCommand Name: reply with meeting

Description: Performs the Outlook "Reply with Meeting" function

Group: Dragon – Microsoft Outlook Step-by-Step commands

Availability: Application-specific

Application: Microsoft Outlook

Command Type: Step-by-Step

Steps:

```
Keystrokes Press Ctrl + Alt + R
Keystrokes Press Alt + T
```

Figure 6-1

The MyCommands Editor window, displaying the configuration for the "reply with meeting" command and its required steps.

Make sure MS Outlook is the active window, select an email and try it by saying:

"reply with meeting"

Discuss

This command uses Outlook keyboard shortcuts to open a new window and select the desired meeting details. First, it uses a **Keystroke** step to perform the keyboard shortcut **Ctrl+Alt+R**, which opens the meeting window. Next, it uses another **Keystroke** step to select the Start Date field by pressing **Alt+T**.

This allows you to easily and efficiently set the start date of your meeting without having to manually navigate through the options.

Turning On Out of Office Replies with a Voice Command

Scenario

You frequently activate your "Out of Office" automatic replies in Microsoft Outlook when you're unavailable. Instead of manually navigating through Outlook menus to enable this feature, you want a streamlined solution. By saying "turn on out of office" Dragon executes a **Step-by-Step** command that performs the required steps to enable your automatic replies efficiently, saving you time and effort.

MyCommand Name: turn on out of office

Description: Turns on the Out of Office feature in Outlook

Group: Dragon – Microsoft Outlook Step-by-Step commands

Availability: Application-specific

Application: Microsoft Outlook

Command Type: Step-by-Step

Steps:

```
Keystrokes Press Alt + F
Send Keys Send Keys "I"
Send Keys Send Keys "O"
Send Keys Send Keys "S"
Keystrokes Press Enter
```

Figure 6-2

The MyCommands Editor window, displaying the configuration for the "turn on out of office" command and its required steps.

Make sure MS Outlook is the active window, and try it by saying:

"turn on out of office"

Discuss

This command involves several steps to automate the process of turning on Out of Office replies in Outlook. First, a **Keystrokes** step executes the keyboard shortcut **Alt+F**, opening the Outlook File menu and ensuring the command works regardless of the current menu. In the File menu, Outlook provides Key Tips for available shortcuts, such as the letter **I** for the Info option.

Next, a **Send Keys** step presses **I** to access the Info options, followed by another **Send Keys** step to press **O** to select the Automatic Replies option. To enable the "Send automatic replies" feature, a **Send Keys** step presses **S**. Finally, a **Keystrokes** step presses the **Enter** key to confirm and complete the process.

Flag the Selected Email for Tomorrow with a Reminder

Scenario

You're a busy professional who receives dozens of emails daily, and you struggle to stay on top of tasks and deadlines. Often, you forget to follow up on important emails that require your attention. To solve this, you decide to create a voice command that sets a reminder for an email to follow up on the next day. This way, you can dictate the reminder while reviewing the email, ensuring you don't forget to act.

This voice command automatically sets a reminder for the selected email for the next day.

MyCommand Name: flag for tomorrow

Description: Flags the selected email for tomorrow with a reminder

Group: Dragon – Microsoft Outlook Step-by-Step commands

Availability: Application-specific

Application: Microsoft Outlook

Command Type: Step-by-Step

Steps:

```
Keystrokes Press Ctrl + Shift + G
Type Text Type "Follow up"
Keystrokes Press Tab
Type Text Type "Tomorrow"
Keystrokes Press Tab
Keystrokes Press Alt + R
Keystrokes Press Enter
```

Figure 6-3

The MyCommands Editor window, displaying the configuration for the "flag for tomorrow" command and its required steps.

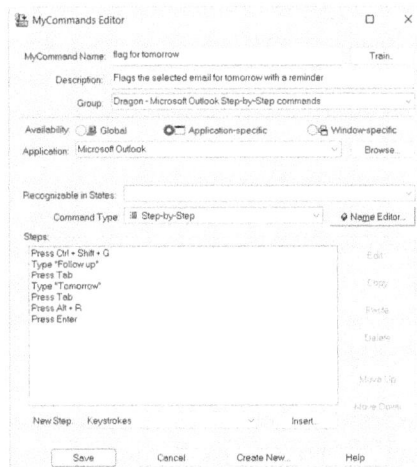

Make sure MS Outlook is the active window, select an email and try it by saying:

"flag for tomorrow"

Discuss

This command is designed to automate the process of flagging an email for follow-up and consists of several steps. First, it uses the keyboard shortcut **Ctrl+Shift+G** to open the **Custom** window. Then, the **Type Text** step is used to insert the flag type, which in this case is **"Follow Up"**.

To confirm the flag type and move to the **Start Date** field, the **Tab** key is pressed using a **Keystrokes** step. After that, the **Type Text** step is used again to enter the keyword for the reminder date, which is **"Tomorrow"**. To confirm the date, a **Keystrokes** step presses the **Tab** key. The keyboard shortcut **Alt+R** is then used to check the reminder checkbox, which is emulated through a **Keystrokes** step. Finally, a **Keystrokes** step is used to simulate pressing the **Enter** key.

Alternative

To modify the scheduled reminder date, simply replace the word "**Tomorrow**" in the **Type Text** step with other options such as "Next Week", "Next Month", "3 Days", "2 Weeks", or even specific dates like "Christmas Day".

Create an Appointment for Two Weeks from Today

Using a sequence of keyboard shortcuts, it is possible to create an appointment for a specific date in the future. However, remembering these shortcuts can be challenging unless you have an exceptional memory.

This **Step-by-Step** command eliminates the need to remember keyboard shortcuts and reduces mouse actions. When executed with the command phrase "create an appointment for two weeks time", Dragon switches to the **Outlook Calendar view**, creates a new appointment, sets the **Start Date** to two weeks from the current date, and finally places the cursor in the **Title** field ready for you to dictate the title.

MyCommand Name: create an appointment for two weeks time

Description: Creates an appointment with the start date automatically set to two weeks from today

Group: Dragon – Microsoft Outlook Step-by-Step commands

Availability: Application-specific

Application: Microsoft Outlook

Command Type: Step-by-Step

Steps:

```
Keystrokes Press Ctrl + 2
Keystrokes Press Ctrl + N
Wait Wait 1000 milliseconds
Keystrokes Press Alt + T
Type Text Type "2 weeks"
Keystrokes Press Tab
Keystrokes Press Alt + L
```

Figure 6-4

The MyCommands Editor window, displaying the configuration for the "create an appointment for two weeks time" command and its required steps.

Make sure MS Outlook is the active window and try it by saying:

"create an appointment for two weeks time"

Discuss

This command consists of several steps. First, it uses a **Keystrokes** step for the keyboard shortcut **Ctrl+2** to switch to the Outlook Calendar view. This ensures that the command functions regardless of the current Outlook view. Another **Keystrokes** step performs the **Ctrl+N** keyboard shortcut, which opens a new, untitled Appointment window.

Next, a **Wait** step is introduced to create a brief delay, allowing time for the Appointment window to open fully. A **Keystrokes** step then selects the **Start time** field, which is populated with the text "**2 weeks**" using the **Type Text** step.

Finally, two additional **Keystrokes** steps confirm the entry and move the cursor to the **Title** field, preparing it for the user to input the appointment title.

Alternative

To modify the appointment date, simply replace the word "**2 weeks**" in the **Type Text** step with other options such as "Next Week", "Next Month", "3 Days", "3 Weeks", or even specific dates like "New Years Eve".

> You may need to adjust the Wait time to accommodate your computer's processing speed to ensure the command works successfully.

Navigate to the Next Appointment in the Outlook Calendar

Scenario

To improve your calendar navigation efficiency, you require a voice command that enable you to navigate between your previous and next appointments.

This Step-by-Step command allows you to dictate a voice command to move to the next appointment in your calendar. You can easily copy and modify it to create a similar command for navigating to the previous appointment.

MyCommand Name: go to next appointment

Description: Moves to the next appointment in the calendar

Group: Dragon – Microsoft Outlook Step-by-Step commands

Availability: Application-specific

Application: Microsoft Outlook

Command Type: Step-by-Step

Steps:

Keystrokes Press Ctrl + Shift + .

Figure 6-5

The MyCommands Editor window, displaying the configuration for the "go to next appointment" command and its required steps.

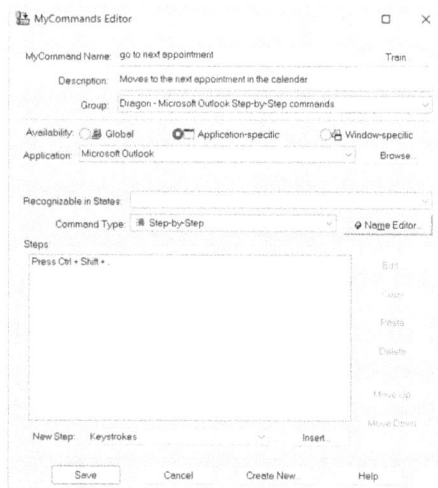

Make sure you are in the MS Outlook Calendar view and try it by saying:

"go to next appointment"

Discuss

This command makes use of keyboard shortcut **Ctrl+Shift+.** (full stop) to move to the next appointment in the calendar. A **Keystroke** step is used to carry out the keyboard shortcut.

Alternative

A similar command that will move you to the previous appointment in the calendar can be created by modifying the **Keystroke** step and changing the details to **Ctrl+Shift+,** (comma). Be sure to update the **MyCommand Name** field with an appropriate command phrase.

Navigate to One Week Before Today's Date in the Outlook Calendar

By default, Dragon does not offer specific voice commands for navigating days within the Outlook calendar. However, Microsoft Outlook provides keyboard shortcuts that can be utilised to create custom, memorable voice commands for this purpose.

This Step-by-Step command allows you to use the voice command phrase "go to previous week" to navigate to the date one week prior to today's date.

MyCommand Name: go to previous week

Description: Moves to the week before today's date in the calendar

Group: Dragon – Microsoft Outlook Step-by-Step commands

Availability: Application-specific

Application: Microsoft Outlook

Command Type: Step-by-Step

Steps:

Keystrokes Press Alt + Up

Figure 6-6

The MyCommands Editor window, displaying the configuration for the "go to previous week" command and its required steps.

Ensure you're in the MS Outlook Calendar, viewing today's date, and try saying:

"go to previous week"

Discuss

This command makes use of keyboard shortcut **Alt+Up Arrow** to move to the previous week. A **Keystroke** step is used to carry out the keyboard shortcut.

Alternative

A similar command that will move you to the following week can be created by modifying the **Keystroke** step and changing the details to **Alt+Down Arrow**. Be sure to update the **MyCommand Name** field with an appropriate command phrase.

Section 7: Dragon Commands for Microsoft Excel

Dragon Commands for Microsoft Excel

The Dragon application works seamlessly with Microsoft Excel right out of the box, as indicated by the Full Text Control Indicator (a small green light in the DragonBar). It supports a range of voice commands, from basic navigation within spreadsheets to advanced tasks like creating charts.

This section introduces several bespoke commands not included in Dragon's default setup. These commands are designed to enhance productivity when using Microsoft Excel and have been created and tested with **MS Excel in Office 365**.

These macros are also compatible with earlier versions of MS Excel.

In This Part: Step-by-Step Commands

38–45

Autofit the Width of an Excel Cell

By default, Dragon does not provide a specific voice command to autofit a cell's width to its content. However, since this task can be performed using a series of keyboard shortcuts, a **Step-by-Step** command can be created to accomplish it by voice, thereby reducing the need for mouse and keyboard actions.

This **Step-by-Step** command allows you to use the voice command phrase "autofit cell width" to adjust the cell width to match its content.

MyCommand Name: autofit cell width

Description: Autofits an Excel cell width

Group: Dragon – Microsoft Excel Step-by-Step commands

Availability: Application-specific

Application: Microsoft Excel

Command Type: Step-by-Step

Steps:

```
Keystrokes Press Alt + H
Send Keys Send Keys "o"
Send Keys Send Keys "i"
```

Figure 7-0

The MyCommands Editor window, displaying the configuration for the "autofit cell width" command and its required steps.

Ensure MS Excel is the active window, select a cell, and try it by saying:

"autofit cell width"

Discuss

This command consists of several steps to automate the process of autofitting the cell width. First, a **Keystrokes** step uses the keyboard shortcut **Alt+H** to access the Excel Home menu. Next, two **Send Keys** steps are used to press the letters **O** and then **I**, completing the autofit action.

Autofit the Height of an Excel Cell

By default, Dragon does not provide a specific voice command to autofit a cell's height to its content. However, since this task can be performed using a series of keyboard shortcuts, a **Step-by-Step** command can be created to accomplish it by voice, thereby reducing the need for mouse and keyboard actions.

This **Step-by-Step** command allows you to use the voice command phrase "autofit cell height" to adjust the cell height to match its content.

MyCommand Name: autofit cell height

Description: Autofits an Excel cell height

Group: Dragon – Microsoft Excel Step-by-Step commands

Availability: Application-specific

Application: Microsoft Excel

Command Type: Step-by-Step

Steps:

```
Keystrokes Press Alt + H
Send Keys Send Keys "o"
Send Keys Send Keys "a"
```

Figure 7-1

The MyCommands Editor window, displaying the configuration for the "autofit cell height" command and its required steps.

Ensure MS Excel is the active window, select a cell, and try it by saying:

"autofit cell height"

Discuss

This command consists of several steps to automate the process of autofitting the cell height. First, a **Keystrokes** step uses the keyboard shortcut **Alt+H** to access the Excel Home menu. Next, two **Send Keys** steps are used to press the letters **O** and then **A**, completing the autofit action.

Apply Wrap Text and Merge & Center to a Cell

Scenario

When working on your Excel spreadsheets, you may often need to format text by applying the **Wrap Text** feature followed by the **Merge & Center** option. To eliminate this repetitive task, you can create a voice command to perform these actions.

This **Step-by-Step** command allows you to use the voice command phrase "wrap text and merge center" to complete the task by voice.

MyCommand Name: wrap text and merge center

Description: Performs wrap text and merge & center functions

Group: Dragon – Microsoft Excel Step-by-Step commands

Availability: Application-specific

Application: Microsoft Excel

Command Type: Step-by-Step

Steps:

```
Keystrokes Press Alt + H
Send Keys Send Keys "w"
Keystrokes Press Alt + H
Send Keys Send Keys "m"
Send Keys Send Keys "c"
```

Figure 7-2

The MyCommands Editor window, displaying the configuration for the "wrap text and merge center" command and its required steps.

Ensure MS Excel is the active window, select a cell or range of cells, and try it by saying:

"wrap text and merge center"

Discuss

This command automates the process of applying the **Wrap Text** feature and the **Merge & Center** option to the selected cell(s). First, a **Keystrokes** step uses the keyboard shortcut **Alt+H** to access the Excel Home menu. Next, a **Send Keys** step presses the letter **W** to wrap the text. Another **Keystrokes** step accesses the Home menu again, followed by two **Send Keys** steps to press **M** and **C**, completing the task by applying **Merge & Center**.

Rotate Text Clockwise in Excel (List command)

By default, Dragon does not provide a specific voice command to rotate text diagonally or vertically—a useful feature for labelling narrow columns in Excel sheets. However, this task can be performed using a series of keyboard shortcuts, allowing you to create a Step-by-Step command to execute these options by voice.

This **Step-by-Step List** command enables you rotate the text in the selected cell(s) to a clockwise angle by dictating any of the following command phrases: "angle text clockwise" or "rotate clockwise".

MyCommand Name: <excel_rotate_text_clockwise>

Name of List(s) used: <excel_rotate_text_clockwise>

List items:
angle text clockwise
rotate clockwise

Description: Rotates the text to an angle clockwise

Group: Dragon – Microsoft Excel Step-by-Step commands

Availability: Application-specific

Application: Microsoft Excel

Command Type: Step-by-Step

Steps:

```
Keystrokes Press Alt + H
Send Keys Send Keys "f"
Send Keys Send Keys "q"
Send Keys Send Keys "l"
```

Figure 7-3

The MyCommands Editor window, displaying the configuration for the "<excel_rotate_text_clockwise>" command and its required steps.

Ensure MS Excel is the active window, select a cell or range of cells, and try it by saying:

"angle text clockwise"

Discuss

This command starts with a **Keystrokes** step to perform the keyboard shortcut **Alt+H** which opens the Excel Home menu. Next, **Send Keys** steps are used to press the letters **F**, **Q**, and **L** sequentially, selecting the **Angle Clockwise** option.

To facilitate dictation of natural language variations to rotate the text, we have created a Dragon List command. The List named <excel_rotate_text_clockwise> contains all the voice command phrases that can be dictated to execute the command. You can add alternative command phrases to execute the command by editing the List.

Adding a Comment to an Excel Cell

By default, Dragon does not provide a specific voice command to open the comments window for adding a comment to a cell. However, since this task can be accomplished using a series of keyboard key presses, a **Step-by-Step** command can be created to perform the action by voice.

Figure 7-4

Figure 7-4 shows a Comments window positioned next to a cell in an Excel spreadsheet.

This **Step-by-Step** command allows you to use the voice command phrase "insert a comment" to open the comments window, ready for you to dictate your comment.

MyCommand Name: insert a comment

Description: Add a Comment to an Excel Cell

Group: Dragon – Microsoft Excel Step-by-Step commands

Availability: Application-specific

Application: Microsoft Excel

Command Type: Step-by-Step

Steps:

```
Keystrokes Press Alt + N
Send Keys Send Keys "C"
Send Keys Send Keys "M"
```

Figure 7-5

The MyCommands Editor window, displaying the configuration for the "insert a comment" command and its required steps.

Ensure MS Excel is the active window, select a cell, and try it by saying:

"insert a comment"

Discuss

This command consists of several steps to open the Comments window. First, a **Keystrokes** step uses the keyboard shortcut **Alt+N** to access the Excel **Insert** menu. Next, two **Send Keys** steps are used: the first presses the letter **C** and the second presses the letter **M**.

Removing Hyperlinks in Excel Cells (List command)

When copying and pasting links into your spreadsheets, you'll often find that the links are active. Selecting and editing cells containing active links can be a nuisance, as you may inadvertently be redirected to the link destination. To avoid this, one solution is to remove the hyperlink properties from the cells in the worksheet.

However, removing the active links would typically involve navigating through all the links in a worksheet or workbook and manually removing the hyperlink properties for each cell. This can be a lengthy process.

This **Step-by-Step List** command removes the hyperlink properties from the selected cells by dictating any of the following command phrases: "remove the hyperlinks" or "remove hyperlink".

MyCommand Name: <excel_remove_hyperlinks>

Name of List(s) used: <excel_remove_hyperlinks>

List items:
remove hyperlink
remove the hyperlinks

Description: Removes Hyperlinks from cells

Group: Dragon – Microsoft Excel Step-by-Step commands

Availability: Application-specific

Application: Microsoft Excel

Command Type: Step-by-Step

Steps:

Keystrokes Press Shift + F10
Send Keys Send Keys "r"

Figure 7-6

The MyCommands Editor window, displaying the configuration for the "<excel_remove_hyperlinks>" command and its required steps.

Ensure MS Excel is the active window, select a cell or range of cells, and try it by saying:

"remove the hyperlinks"

Discuss

First, a **Keystrokes** step uses the keyboard shortcut **Shift+F10** to emulate clicking the right mouse button to reveal a menu. Next, a **Send Keys** step is used to press the letter **R** to remove the hyperlinks.

To facilitate dictation of natural language variations for removing the hyperlinks, we have created a Dragon List command. The List named <excel_remove_hyperlinks> contains all the voice command phrases that can be dictated to execute the command. You can add alternative command phrases to execute the command by editing the List.

Highlight All Duplicates in the Selected Range

If you have ever set up a formula and conditional formatting to highlight duplicates in your spreadsheet data, you will be only too aware of how frustrating this can be; it takes up an enormous amount of time and requires maintenance where values might change.

This **Step-by-Step** command offers a solution: simply highlight a range of data, dictate the voice command "highlight duplicates in selection" and have all the duplicates within the range highlighted.

Figure 7-7

	A	B	C	D
1	Name	Surname	Age	Occupation
2	Joe	Blogs	21	Carpenter
3	Victoria	Morris	37	Teacher
4	David	Brown	32	Plumber
5	Mike	Lloyd	50	Artist
6	Oswald	Smith	60	Artist
7	David	Brown	32	Plumber
8	Lydia	Jones	27	Doctor
9	Jane	Mead	29	Nurse
10	Victoria	Morris	37	Teacher

	A	B	C	D
1	Name	Surname	Age	Occupation
2	Joe	Blogs	21	Carpenter
3	Victoria	Morris	37	Teacher
4	David	Brown	32	Plumber
5	Mike	Lloyd	50	Artist
6	Oswald	Smith	60	Artist
7	David	Brown	32	Plumber
8	Lydia	Jones	27	Doctor
9	Jane	Mead	29	Nurse
10	Victoria	Morris	37	Teacher

Figure 7-7 shows how a selected range of data will be transformed by highlighting all duplicate data.

MyCommand Name: highlight duplicates in selection

Description: Highlights the duplicates in the selected range

Group: Dragon – Microsoft Excel Step-by-Step commands

Availability: Application-specific

Application: Microsoft Excel

Command Type: Step-by-Step

Steps:

```
Keystrokes Press Alt + H
Send Keys Send Keys "l"
Send Keys Send Keys "h"
Send Keys Send Keys "d"
Send Keys Send Keys "d"
Keystrokes Press Tab
Send Keys Send Keys "y"
Keystrokes Press Enter
```

Figure 7-8

The MyCommands Editor window, displaying the configuration for the "highlight duplicates in selection" command and its required steps.

Ensure MS Excel is the active window, select a range of cells, and try it by saying:

"highlight duplicates in selection"

Discuss

This command consists of several steps to highlight duplicates within a range of cells. First, a **Keystrokes** step uses the keyboard shortcut **Alt+H** to access the Excel Home menu. The next three steps use **Send Keys** steps to navigate to and open the Duplicate Values window. The fourth step uses a **Send Keys** step to press the letter **D**, ensuring the "Duplicate" option is selected.

Next, to select the type of formatting, a **Keystrokes** step is used to press the **Tab** key, followed by a **Send Keys** step to press the **Y** key, selecting the "Yellow Fill with Dark Yellow Text" option. Finally, a **Keystrokes** step is used to press the **Enter** key to complete the task.

Alternative

You can change the formatting style by modifying the letter in the seventh step. For example, changing **Send Keys** "**Y**" to **Send Keys** "**G**" will style the duplicates with a green fill and dark green text.

Insert the Days of the Week

Scenario

As part of your work, you frequently need to create spreadsheets with the days of the week as column headings. Typically, this involves manually typing each day and dragging across the row with your mouse, or navigating through Excel's menus to use the Series feature. Both methods can be time-consuming and repetitive.

A simple voice command can streamline this process. When executed, the days of the week instantly appear as column headers starting from the selected cell, saving you time and effort while increasing efficiency.

This **Step-by-Step** command is designed to achieve precisely that, allowing you to populate the days of the week horizontally with ease.

MyCommand Name: insert the days of the week

Description: Insert the days of the week from the current cell to the right

Group: Dragon – Microsoft Excel Step-by-Step commands

Availability: Application-specific

Application: Microsoft Excel

Command Type: Step-by-Step

Steps:

```
Type Text Type "Monday"
Keystrokes Press Right
Type Text Type "Tuesday"
Keystrokes Press Right
Type Text Type "Wednesday"
Keystrokes Press Right
Type Text Type "Thursday"
Keystrokes Press Right
Type Text Type "Friday"
Keystrokes Press Right
Type Text Type "Saturday"
Keystrokes Press Right
Type Text Type "Sunday"
Keystrokes Press Right
```

Figure 7-9

The MyCommands Editor window, displaying the configuration for the "insert the days of the week" command and its required steps.

Ensure MS Excel is the active window, select a cell, and try it by saying:

"insert the days of the week"

Discuss

This command consists of several similar steps. **Type Text** steps are used to insert the days, and **Keystrokes** steps are used to move the selection to the cell on the right.

Dragon Commands for Microsoft PowerPoint

By default, Dragon offers only basic text control with MS PowerPoint, as indicated by the Full Text Control Indicator (the small green light) being turned off in the DragonBar. Typical commands include the ability to create slides, navigate around the presentation, and switch between different views.

This section provides several useful Step-by-Step commands that are not available with Dragon out of the box. These commands will enhance the way you work with MS PowerPoint by voice. They have been created and tested using **MS PowerPoint Office 365** but can also be used with earlier versions of MS PowerPoint.

In This Part: Step-by-Step Commands 46–55

Navigating the PowerPoint Panes (List command)

By default, Dragon does not include a voice command to navigate between panes in PowerPoint presentations. However, PowerPoint offers keyboard shortcuts for this functionality, allowing us to create **Step-by-Step** commands with easy-to-remember voice command phrases.

This **Step-by-Step List** command enables you to move to the next pane by saying either "next pane" or "move to next pane".

MyCommand Name: <move to next pane>

Name of List(s) used: <move to next pane>

List items:
next pane
move to next pane

Description: Makes the next pane become the active pane

Group: Dragon – Microsoft PowerPoint Step-by-Step commands

Availability: Application-specific

Application: Microsoft PowerPoint

Command Type: Step-by-Step

Steps:

`Keystrokes` Press F6

Figure 8-0

The MyCommands Editor window, displaying the configuration for the "<move to next pane>" command and its required steps.

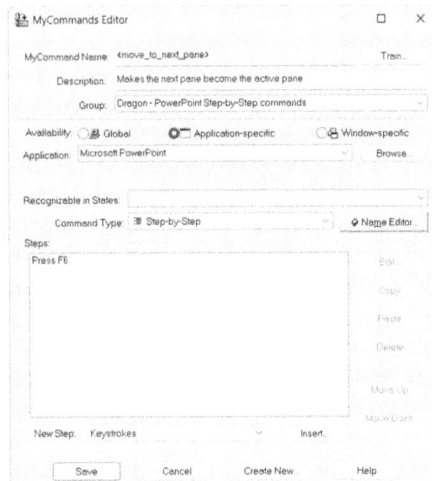

Make sure MS PowerPoint is the active window and try it by saying:

"move to next pane"

Discuss

The PowerPoint keyboard shortcut to move to the next pane is **F6**, so a **Keystrokes** step is used to emulate pressing the **F6** key.

To allow for natural language variations when dictating this command, we created a Dragon List command. The List, named <move to next pane>, contains all the voice command phrases that can trigger the command. You can edit the List to add alternative phrases for executing the command.

Alternative

A similar command that will move you to the previous pane can be created by modifying the **Keystroke** step and changing the details to **Shift+F6**. Be sure to update the **MyCommand Name** field with an appropriate command phrase.

Rotate the Selected Object(s) 90 Degrees Clockwise

By default, Dragon does not provide a specific voice command to rotate the selected object(s) clockwise 90 degrees. However, since this task can be performed using a series of keyboard shortcuts, a **Step-by-Step** command can be created to accomplish it by voice, thereby reducing the need for mouse and keyboard actions.

This **Step-by-Step** command allows you to use the voice command phrase "rotate clockwise ninety degrees" to rotate the selected object(s) 90 degrees to the right.

MyCommand Name: rotate clockwise ninety degrees

Description: Rotates the selected object(s) clockwise 90 degrees

Group: Dragon – Microsoft PowerPoint Step-by-Step commands

Availability: Application-specific

Application: Microsoft PowerPoint

Command Type: Step-by-Step

Steps:

```
Keystrokes Press Alt + H
Send Keys Send Keys "G"
Send Keys Send Keys "O"
Send Keys Send Keys "R"
```

Figure 8-1

The MyCommands Editor window, displaying the configuration for the "rotate clockwise ninety degrees" command and its required steps.

Ensure that MS PowerPoint is the active window, select one or more objects, and try it by saying:
"rotate clockwise ninety degrees"

Discuss

This command consists of several steps to rotate the selected object(s). First, a **Keystrokes** step uses the keyboard shortcut **Alt+H** to access the PowerPoint Home menu. Next, three **Send Keys** steps are used to press the letters **G**, **O**, and **R**, completing the rotate action.

> When deciding on a command phrase that includes a number. It is best practice to write the number in word form rather than using the numeral.

Changing the Fill Colour of Selected Object(s) to a Specific Hex Value (List command)

Scenario

When creating PowerPoint presentations, you often need to fill shapes with a specific Hex colour. Instead of repeatedly accessing the PowerPoint menus and manually entering the value, you need a voice command to perform the task for you.

This **Step-by-Step List** command changes the fill colour of the selected object(s) to the Hex value #ef8839, reducing the need for repetitive mouse and keyboard actions and minimising the risk of mistakes when done manually.

MyCommand Name: <apply my fill colour>

Name of List(s) used: <apply my fill colour>

List items:

apply my fill colour

change to custom fill colour

Description: Changes the fill colour of the selected object(s)

Group: Dragon – Microsoft PowerPoint Step-by-Step commands

Availability: Application-specific

Application: Microsoft PowerPoint

Command Type: Step-by-Step

Steps:

```
Keystrokes  Press Alt + H
Send Keys   Send Keys "s"
Send Keys   Send Keys "f"
Send Keys   Send Keys "m"
Keystrokes  Press Alt + H
Type Text   Type "#ef8839"
Keystrokes  Press Enter
```

Figure 8-2

The MyCommands Editor window, displaying the configuration for the "<apply my fill colour>" command and its required steps.

Ensure that MS PowerPoint is the active window, select one or more objects, and try it by saying:
"apply my fill colour"

Discuss

This command consists of several steps to change the fill colour of the selected object(s). First, a **Keystrokes** step uses the keyboard shortcut **Alt+H** to access the PowerPoint Home menu. Next, three **Send Keys** steps are used to press the letters **S**, **F**, and **M** to open the **Colors** window. Carrying out the keyboard shortcut **Alt+H** will select the **Hex** field, so a **Keystrokes** step is used at this point. Then, a **Type Text** step is used to insert the hex value, and finally, a **Keystrokes** step is used to press the **Enter** key to complete the action.

To facilitate dictation of natural language variations for changing the fill colour, we have created a Dragon List command. The List named <apply my fill colour> contains all the voice command phrases that can be dictated to execute the command. You can add alternative command phrases to execute the command by editing the List.

> Microsoft PowerPoint enhances accessibility by indicating available keyboard shortcuts. For example, you can navigate to the Hex field using Alt+H, as the underlined H in the field title serves as a visual cue for this shortcut.

Alternative

You can change the Hex value by editing the **Type Text** step and entering a different hexadecimal code.

Applying a Specific PowerPoint Animation to Objects

Scenario

When creating PowerPoint presentations, you often need to apply specific animations to objects. Instead of repeatedly navigating menus and manually configuring animation settings, a voice command can streamline the process.

This **Step-by-Step** command applies the "Fly In" animation to the selected object(s), reducing repetitive mouse and keyboard actions while minimising the risk of errors from manual repetition.

MyCommand Name: add fly in animation

Description: Adds the default fly in animation to the selected object(s)

Group: Dragon – Microsoft PowerPoint Step-by-Step commands

Availability: Application-specific

Application: Microsoft PowerPoint

Command Type: Step-by-Step

Steps:

```
Keystrokes Press Alt + A
Send Keys Send Keys "A"
Send Keys Send Keys "A"
Send Keys Send Keys "{Right 2}"
Keystrokes Press Enter
```

Figure 8-3

The MyCommands Editor window, displaying the configuration for the "add fly in animation" command and its required steps.

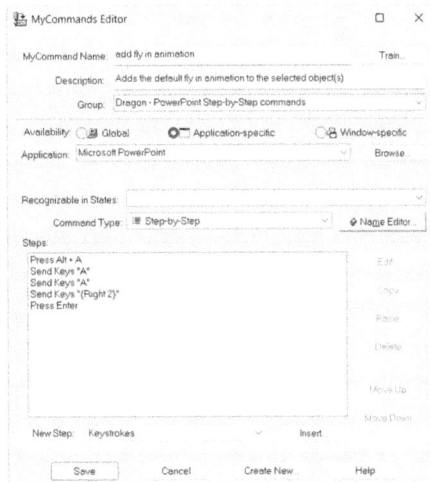

Ensure that MS PowerPoint is the active window, select one or more objects, and try it by saying:
"add fly in animation"

Discuss

This command consists of several steps to apply the animation to the selected object(s). First, a **Keystrokes** step uses the keyboard shortcut **Alt+A** to open the PowerPoint Animations menu. Next, two **Send Keys** steps are used to press the letter **A** twice. To select the "Fly In" option, the **Right Arrow** key is pressed twice, achieved by using a **Send Keys** step with the code {Right 2}. Finally, a **Keystrokes** step presses the **Enter** key to confirm the selection.

When inserting the text within the "Send Keys" step, it is important to include a space after the code and before the value such as in {Right 2}.

Showing or Hiding the PowerPoint Animation Pane (List command)

By default, Dragon does not provide specific voice commands to show or hide the Animation Pane. However, since this task can be performed using keyboard shortcuts, a **Step-by-Step List** command can be created to execute it by voice.

This **Step-by-Step List** command allows you to use the voice command phrases "show the animation pane" or "hide the animation pane" to toggle between showing or hiding the pane.

MyCommand Name: <show_hide_animation_pane>

Name of List(s) used: <show_hide_animation_pane>

List items:
show the animation pane
hide the animation pane

Description: Show or hides the PowerPoint Animation Pane

Group: Dragon – Microsoft PowerPoint Step-by-Step commands

Availability: Application-specific

Application: Microsoft PowerPoint

Command Type: Step-by-Step

Steps:

```
Keystrokes Press Alt + A
Send Keys Send Keys "C"
```

Figure 8-4

The MyCommands Editor window, displaying the configuration for the "<show_hide_animation_pane>" command and its required steps.

Ensure that MS PowerPoint is the active window and try it by saying:

"show the animation pane"
"hide the animation pane"

Discuss

The Animation Pane can be revealed using the keyboard shortcut **Alt+A,** followed by pressing the letter **C.** Therefore, we first use a **Keystrokes** step to emulate **Alt+A** and a **Send Keys** step to emulate pressing the letter **C.**

As it is the same keyboard shortcut to show or hide the pane, we create a Dragon List command to allow for natural language variations. The List, named `<show_hide_animation_pane>`, contains all the voice command phrases that can trigger the command. You can edit the List to add alternative phrases for executing the command.

Previewing the Animations on a Slide

By default, Dragon does not provide a specific voice command to preview animations on the active slide. However, since this task can be performed using keyboard shortcuts, a **Step-by-Step** command can be created to execute it by voice.

This **Step-by-Step** command allows you to use the voice command phrase "preview slide animations" to preview the animations on the active slide.

MyCommand Name: preview slide animations

Description: Runs a preview of the animations on the selected slide

Group: Dragon – Microsoft PowerPoint Step-by-Step commands

Availability: Application-specific

Application: Microsoft PowerPoint

Command Type: Step-by-Step

Steps:

```
Keystrokes Press Alt + A
Send Keys Send Keys "P"
Send Keys Send Keys "P"
```

Figure 8-5

The MyCommands Editor window, displaying the configuration for the "preview slide animations" command and its required steps.

Ensure that MS PowerPoint is the active window, select a slide with animations and try it by saying:
"preview slide animations"

Discuss

To review the animations, we can use the keyboard shortcut **Alt+A,** followed by pressing the letter **P** twice. Therefore, we first use a **Keystrokes** step to emulate **Alt+A** and then use two **Send Keys** steps to emulate pressing the letter **P** twice.

Showing or Hiding the Selection Pane (List command)

By default, Dragon does not provide specific voice commands to show or hide the Selection Pane. However, since this task can be performed using a keyboard shortcut, a **Step-by-Step List** command can be created to execute the action by voice.

This **Step-by-Step List** command allows you to use the voice command phrases "show the selection pane" or "hide the selection pane" to toggle between showing or hiding the pane.

MyCommand Name: <show_hide_selection_pane>

Name of List(s) used: <show_hide_selection_pane>

List items:
show the selection pane
hide the selection pane

Description: Shows or hides the selection pane

Group: Dragon – Microsoft PowerPoint Step-by-Step commands

Availability: Application-specific

Application: Microsoft PowerPoint

Command Type: Step-by-Step

Steps:

`Keystrokes Press Alt + F10`

Figure 8-6

The MyCommands Editor window, displaying the configuration for the "<show_hide_selection_pane>" command and its required steps.

Ensure that MS PowerPoint is the active window and try it by saying:

"show the selection pane"
"hide the selection pane"

Discuss

The Selection Pane can be revealed using the keyboard shortcut **Alt+F10**. Therefore, we use a **Keystrokes** step to emulate **Alt+F10**.

As it is the same keyboard shortcut to show or hide the pane, we create a Dragon List command to allow for natural language variations. The List, named `<show_hide_selection_pane>`, contains all the voice command phrases that can trigger the command. You can edit the List to add alternative phrases for executing the command.

Switch To Eyedropper Tool

By default, Dragon does not provide a specific voice command to switch to the PowerPoint Eyedropper Tool. However, since this task can be performed using keyboard shortcuts, a **Step-by-Step** command can be created to open the tool by voice.

This **Step-by-Step** command allows you to use the voice command phrase "open eye dropper tool" to switch to the tool.

MyCommand Name: open eye dropper tool

Description: Opens the Eyedropper Tool

Group: Dragon – Microsoft PowerPoint Step-by-Step commands

Availability: Application-specific

Application: Microsoft PowerPoint

Command Type: Step-by-Step

Steps:

```
Keystrokes Press Alt + H
Send Keys Send Keys "F"
Send Keys Send Keys "C"
Send Keys Send Keys "E"
```

Figure 8-7

The MyCommands Editor window, displaying the configuration for the "open eye dropper tool" command and its required steps.

Ensure that MS PowerPoint is the active window, select an object and try it by saying:
"open eye dropper tool"

Discuss

To open the Eyedropper Tool, we can use the keyboard shortcut **Alt+H,** followed by pressing the letters **F, C** and **E** in sequence. Therefore, we first use a **Keystrokes** step to emulate **Alt+H** and then three **Send Keys** steps to emulate pressing the letters **F, C** and **E**.

Adding a Specific Transition to a PowerPoint Slide

Scenario

When creating PowerPoint presentations, you often need to apply specific transition effects to slides. Instead of repeatedly navigating through menus and manually configuring transition settings, a voice command can streamline the process.

This **Step-by-Step** command applies the "Shape" transition to the active slide, reducing repetitive mouse and keyboard actions while minimising the risk of errors from manual repetition.

MyCommand Name: add the shape transition

Description: Adds the default shape transition effect to the active slide

Group: Dragon – Microsoft PowerPoint Step-by-Step commands

Availability: Application-specific

Application: Microsoft PowerPoint

Command Type: Step-by-Step

Steps:

```
Keystrokes  Press Alt + K
Send Keys   Send Keys "T"
Send Keys   Send Keys "{Right 9}"
Keystrokes  Press Enter
```

Figure 8-8

The MyCommands Editor window, displaying the configuration for the "add the shape transition" command and its required steps.

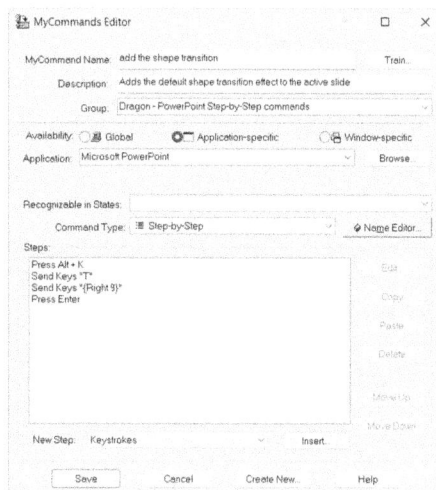

Ensure that MS PowerPoint is the active window, select a slide and try it by saying:
"add the shape transition"

Discuss

This command consists of several steps to apply the transition effect to the active slide. First, a **Keystrokes** step uses the keyboard shortcut **Alt+K** to open the PowerPoint Transitions menu. Next, a **Send Keys** step is used to press the letter **T**. To select the "Shape" option, the **Right Arrow** key is pressed nine times, achieved by using a **Send Keys** step with the code `{Right 9}`. Finally, a **Keystrokes** step presses the **Enter** key to confirm the selection.

> When inserting the text within the "Send Keys" step, it is important to include a space after the code and before the value such as in {Right 9}.

Setting a Specific Transition Duration for a PowerPoint Slide

Scenario

When creating PowerPoint presentations, you often need to change the default duration of slide transitions. Rather than repeatedly navigating menus and manually adjusting transition settings, a voice command can simplify the process.

This **Step-by-Step** command sets the transition duration to five seconds on the active slide, streamlining the process and reducing the risk of errors from repetitive mouse and keyboard actions.

MyCommand Name: change the transition duration

Description: Changes the slide transition duration to 5 seconds

Group: Dragon – Microsoft PowerPoint Step-by-Step commands

Availability: Application-specific

Application: Microsoft PowerPoint

Command Type: Step-by-Step

Steps:

```
Keystrokes  Press Alt + K
Send Keys   Send Keys "E"
Type Text   Type "5"
Keystrokes  Press Enter
```

Figure 8-9

The MyCommands Editor window, displaying the configuration for the "change the transition duration" command and its required steps.

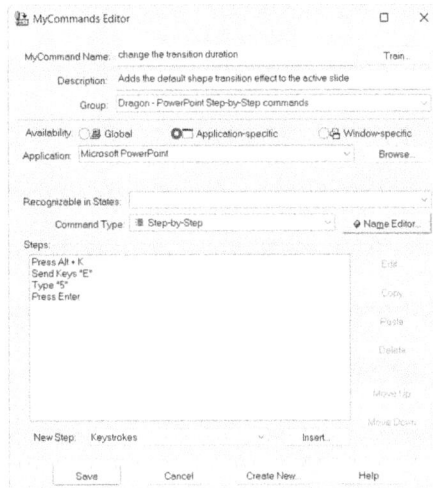

Ensure that MS PowerPoint is the active window, select a slide and try it by saying:
"change the transition duration"

Discuss

This command consists of several steps to set the transition duration time. First, a **Keystrokes** step uses the keyboard shortcut **Alt+K** to open the PowerPoint Transitions menu. Next, a **Send Keys** step is used to press the letter **E** to select the Duration field. A **Type Text** step is then used to insert the desired value. Finally, a **Keystrokes** step presses the **Enter** key to confirm the entry.

Dragon Commands for Microsoft Publisher

Dragon, by default, offers basic text control for the Microsoft Publisher application, as indicated by the Full Text Control Indicator (a small green indicator) being turned off in the DragonBar. While most MS Publisher functions can be performed by dictating key presses, this approach requires memorising all the available shortcut keystrokes.

This section introduces several useful Step-by-Step commands designed for use with Microsoft Publisher. These commands have been created and tested with **MS Publisher Office 365** and are also compatible with earlier versions of Microsoft Publisher.

In This Part: Step-by-Step Commands 56–65

Switching to the Whole Page View

When working on your Publisher documents you may often need to switch to the whole page view to see an overall picture of the page you are working on.

This **Step-by-Step** command enables you to switch to the whole page view at anytime by dictating the command phrase "switch to whole page view".

MyCommand Name: switch to whole page view

Description: Switches to the Whole Page view

Group: Dragon – Microsoft Publisher Step-by-Step commands

Availability: Application-specific

Application: Microsoft Publisher

Command Type: Step-by-Step

Steps:

Keystrokes Press Ctrl + Shift + L

Figure 9-0

The MyCommands Editor window, displaying the configuration for the "switch to whole page view" command and its required steps.

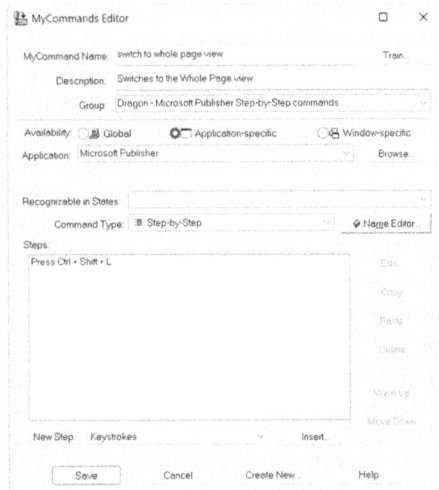

Ensure that MS Publisher is the active window and try it by saying:
"switch to whole page view"

Discuss

Switching to the Whole Page view can be accomplished using the keyboard shortcut **Ctrl+Shift+L**. This command uses a **Keystrokes** step to emulate pressing **Ctrl+Shift+L**.

Alternative

A similar command can be created to switch the view to 100% by modifying the **Keystrokes** step to use **F9**. Be sure to update the **MyCommand Name** field with an appropriate command phrase.

Showing or Hiding the Publisher Rulers (List command)

This **Step-by-Step List** command enables you to toggle the visibility of the Publisher rulers. By simply dictating the voice command phrases "show the rulers" or "hide the rulers" you can display or hide the rulers as needed.

MyCommand Name: <show_hide_rulers>

Name of List(s) used: <show_hide_rulers>

List items:
hide the rulers
show the rulers

Description: Shows and hides the Publisher rulers

Group: Dragon – Microsoft Publisher Step-by-Step commands

Availability: Application-specific

Application: Microsoft Publisher

Command Type: Step-by-Step

Steps:

Keystrokes Press Alt + W
Send Keys Send Keys "R"

Figure 9-1

The MyCommands Editor window, displaying the configuration for the "<show_hide_rulers>" command and its required steps.

Ensure that MS Publisher is the active window and try it by saying:

"hide the rulers

"show the rulers"

Discuss

The Publisher rulers can be revealed or hidden using the keyboard shortcut **Alt+W**, followed by pressing the letter **R**. Therefore, we use a **Keystrokes** step to emulate **Alt+W**, followed by a **Send Keys** step to press the letter **R**.

As it is the same keyboard shortcut to show or hide the rulers, we create a Dragon List command to allow for natural language variations. The List, named <show_hide_rulers>, contains all the voice command phrases that can trigger the command. You can edit the List to add alternative phrases for executing the command.

Showing or Hiding the Publisher Guidelines (List command)

This **Step-by-Step List** command enables you to toggle the visibility of Publisher guidelines. By simply dictating the voice command phrases "show the guidelines" or "hide the guidelines" you can effortlessly display or hide the rulers as needed.

MyCommand Name: <show_hide_guidelines>

Name of List(s) used: <show_hide_guidelines>

List items:
hide the guide lines
show the guide lines

Description: Shows and hides the Publisher guidelines

Group: Dragon – Microsoft Publisher Step-by-Step commands

Availability: Application-specific

Application: Microsoft Publisher

Command Type: Step-by-Step

Steps:

```
Keystrokes Press Alt + W
Send Keys Send Keys "D"
```

Figure 9-2

The MyCommands Editor window, displaying the
configuration for the "<show_hide_guidelines>"
command and its required steps.

Ensure that MS Publisher is the active window and try it by saying:

"hide the guide lines

"show the guide lines"

Discuss

The Publisher rulers can be revealed or hidden using the keyboard shortcut **Alt+W**, followed by pressing the letter **D**. Therefore, we use a **Keystrokes** step to emulate **Alt+W**, followed by a **Send Keys** step to press the letter **D**.

As it is the same keyboard shortcut to show or hide the guidelines, we create a Dragon List command to allow for natural language variations. The List, named <show_hide_guidelines>, contains all the voice command phrases that can trigger the command. You can edit the List to add alternative phrases for executing the command.

Sending Selected Objects to the Back in Publisher

The ability to arrange or layer objects, such as sending them to the back or bringing them to the front, is a fundamental tool when creating Publisher documents.

This **Step-by-Step** command sends the selected object(s) to the back when you dictate the command phrase "send to the back".

MyCommand Name: send to the back

Description: Sends the select object(s) to the back

Group: Dragon – Microsoft Publisher Step-by-Step commands

Availability: Application-specific

Application: Microsoft Publisher

Command Type: Step-by-Step

Steps:

Keystrokes Press Alt + Shift + F6

Figure 9-3

The MyCommands Editor window, displaying the configuration for the "send to the back" command and its required steps.

Ensure that MS Publisher is the active window, select an object(s) and try it by saying:
"send to the back"

Discuss

Sending the selected object(s) to the back can be accomplished using the keyboard shortcut **Alt+Shift+F6**. This command uses a **Keystrokes** step to emulate pressing **Alt+Shift+F6**.

Alternative

A similar command to bring the selected object(s) to the front can be created by modifying the **Keystrokes** step to use **Alt+F6**. Ensure that the **MyCommand Name** field is updated with an appropriate command phrase.

Bringing the Selected Objects Forwards in Publisher (List command)

The ability to arrange or layer objects, such as sending them backward or forward, is an essential feature when creating Publisher documents.

This **Step-by-Step** command brings the selected object(s) forward when you dictate either the command phrase "bring this forward" or "bring these forward".

MyCommand Name: <bring forwards>

Name of List(s) used: <group_ungroup_objects>

List items:
bring this forward
bring these forward

Description: Brings the select object(s) forwards

Group: Dragon – Microsoft Publisher Step-by-Step commands

Availability: Application-specific

Application: Microsoft Publisher

Command Type: Step-by-Step

Steps:

```
Keystrokes Press Alt + H
Send Keys Send Keys "AFF"
```

Figure 9-4

The MyCommands Editor window, displaying the configuration for the "<bring forwards>" command and its required steps.

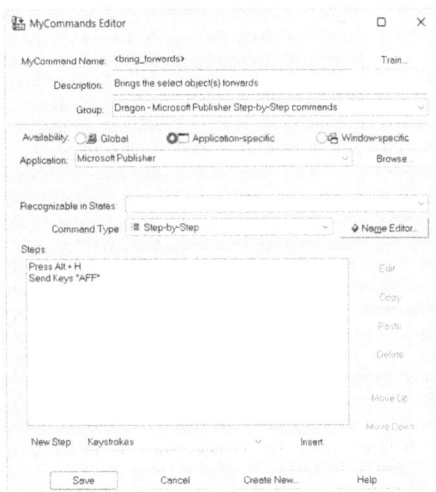

Ensure that MS Publisher is the active window, select an object(s) and try it by saying:

"bring this forward"

"bring these forward"

Discuss

This command begins with a **Keystrokes** step to execute the keyboard shortcut **Alt+H**, switching to the MS Publisher Home menu and ensuring the command functions regardless of the currently active menu. This shortcut also reveals the Key Tips for the Home ribbon, showing that pressing the letters **A**, followed by **A**, and then **F** selects the Bring Forward option. A single **Send Keys** step (`Send Keys "AFF"`) is used to emulate these keypresses in sequence to execute the Bring Forward action.

To facilitate dictation of natural language variations to send the selected object(s) backwards, we have created a Dragon List command. The List named `<bring forwards>` contains all the voice command phrases that can be dictated to execute the command. You can add alternative command phrases to execute the command by editing the List.

Alternative

A similar command to send the selected object(s) backwards can be created by changing the **Send Keys** step to `Send Keys "AEB"`. Ensure that the **MyCommand Name** field is updated with an appropriate command phrase.

Grouping or Ungrouping the Selected Objects (List command)

By default, Dragon does not provide specific voice commands to group or ungroup selected objects in Microsoft Publisher. However, since this task can be performed using a keyboard shortcut, a **Step-by-Step List** command can be created to execute the action by voice.

This **Step-by-Step List** command allows you to use the voice command phrases "group the objects" or "ungroup the objects" to toggle between grouping or ungrouping the selected objects.

MyCommand Name: <group_ungroup_objects>

Name of List(s) used: <group_ungroup_objects>

List items:
group the objects
ungroup the objects

Description: Groups or ungroups the selected objects

Group: Dragon – Microsoft Publisher Step-by-Step commands

Availability: Application-specific

Application: Microsoft Publisher

Command Type: Step-by-Step

Steps:

Keystrokes Press Ctrl + Shift + G

Figure 9-5

The MyCommands Editor window, displaying the configuration for the "<group_ungroup_objects>" command and its required steps.

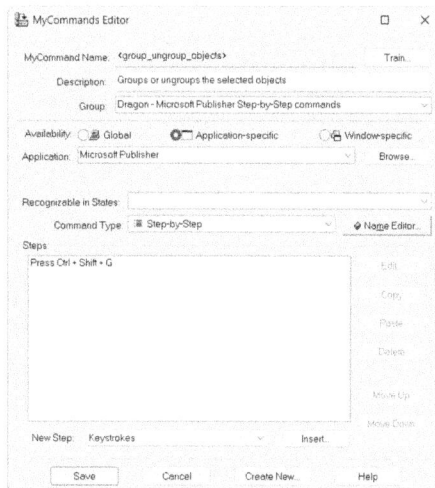

Ensure that MS Publisher is the active window, select some objects and try it by saying:

"group the objects"

"ungroup the objects"

Discuss

Grouping the selected objects can be achieved by using the keyboard shortcut **Ctrl+Shift+G**. Therefore, we use a **Keystrokes** step to emulate pressing **Ctrl+Shift+G**.

As it is the same keyboard shortcut to group or ungroup selected objects, we create a Dragon List command to allow for natural language variations. The List, named `<group_ungroup_objects>`, contains all the voice command phrases that can trigger the command. You can edit the List to add alternative phrases for executing the command.

Streamlining Object Alignment in Publisher

Scenario

You frequently work with Microsoft Publisher to create documents and often need to centrally align objects on the page. However, navigating through menus and manually selecting alignment options each time is time-consuming and repetitive.

This **Step-by-Step** command allows you to centrally align selected objects quickly and accurately. By dictating the command phrase "centrally align these", Dragon will automatically align the objects, saving you time, reducing repetitive actions, and minimise the chance of alignment errors.

MyCommand Name: centrally align these

Description: Centrally aligns the selected objects

Group: Dragon – Microsoft Publisher Step-by-Step commands

Availability: Application-specific

Application: Microsoft Publisher

Command Type: Step-by-Step

Steps:

```
Keystrokes Press Alt + H
Send Keys Send Keys "aac"
```

Figure 9-6

The MyCommands Editor window, displaying the configuration for the "centrally align these" command and its required steps.

Ensure that MS Publisher is the active window, select some objects and try it by saying:

"centrally align these"

Discuss

This command begins with a **Keystrokes** step to execute the keyboard shortcut **Alt+H**, switching to the MS Publisher Home menu and ensuring the command works regardless of the currently active menu. Once the Key Tips for the Home ribbon is revealed, pressing the letters **A**, **A** and **C** will select the Align Center option. Therefore, a single **Send Keys** step is used to emulate pressing the letters **A**, **A**, and **C** in sequence to complete the action.

Move Objects to a Specific Position on the Page

Scenario

In your daily workflow, you frequently need to position objects at specific locations on the page. Manually adjusting the position using the mouse or keyboard can be time-consuming and prone to errors. To streamline this process, you require a voice command where you can simply dictate the command phrase "move to custom position" and Dragon will automatically move the object to the exact coordinates you specify, ensuring precision and saving time.

This **Step-by-Step** command moves the selected object to position 0 cm horizontal and vertical from the top left corner. By dictating the command phrase "move to custom position".

MyCommand Name: move to custom position

Description: Moves the selected object to a specific position

Group: Dragon – Microsoft Publisher Step-by-Step commands

Availability: Application-specific

Application: Microsoft Publisher

Command Type: Step-by-Step

Steps:

```
Keystrokes Press Alt + J
Send Keys Send Keys "DSZ"
Keystrokes Press Right
Keystrokes Press Alt + J
Keystrokes Press Alt + H
Type Text Type "0 cm"
Keystrokes Press Alt + V
Type Text Type "0 cm"
Keystrokes Press Enter
```

Figure 9-7

The MyCommands Editor window, displaying the configuration for the "move to custom position" command and its required steps.

Ensure that MS Publisher is the active window, select an object and try it by saying:

"move to custom position"

Discuss

This command requires an object to be selected first, as this action reveals the Shape Format ribbon.

It begins with a **Keystrokes** step to execute the keyboard shortcut **Alt+J**, switching to the MS Publisher Shape Format menu. Once the Key Tips are revealed, pressing the letters **D**, **S** and **Z** will open the Format Autoshape window. Therefore, a single **Send Keys** step (Send Keys "DSZ") is used to emulate pressing the letters **D**, **S**, and **Z** in sequence to complete the action.

With the Size tab selected by default, a **Keystrokes** step presses the **Right Arrow** key to navigate to the Layout tab. Another **Keystrokes** step uses the keyboard shortcut **Alt+H** to select the Horizontal field, followed by a **Type Text** step to input the value **0 cm**. Similarly, a **Keystrokes** step and a **Type Text** step are used to select the Vertical field and enter the value **0 cm**. Finally, a **Keystrokes** step presses the **Enter** key to complete the process.

Creating Tables in Microsoft Publisher

Unlike when working in Word documents, Dragon does not provide voice commands to generate tables. However, by using a sequence of keyboard shortcuts, you can create tables with specific dimensions.

This **Step-by-Step** command instructs Dragon to create a table with seven columns and three rows.

MyCommand Name: create a seven by three table

Description: Create a table with seven columns and three rows

Group: Dragon – Microsoft Publisher Step-by-Step commands

Availability: Application-specific

Application: Microsoft Publisher

Command Type: Step-by-Step

Steps:

```
Keystrokes Press Alt + H
Send Keys Send Keys "ta"
Send Keys Send Keys "{Right 6}"
Send Keys Send Keys "{Down 2}"
Keystrokes Press Enter
```

Figure 9-8

The MyCommands Editor window, displaying the configuration for the "create a seven by three table" command and its required steps.

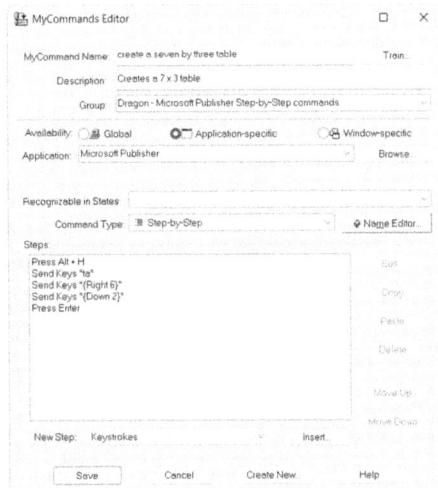

Ensure that MS Publisher is the active window, and try it by saying:
"create a seven by three table"

Discuss

This command begins with a **Keystrokes** step to execute the keyboard shortcut **Alt+H**, switching to the MS Publisher Home menu and ensuring the command works regardless of the currently active menu. This shortcut also reveals the Key Tips for the Home ribbon, indicating that pressing the letter **T** followed by **A** accesses the Table option. A single **Send Keys** step then emulates pressing the Letter **T** followed by **A**

Figure 9-9

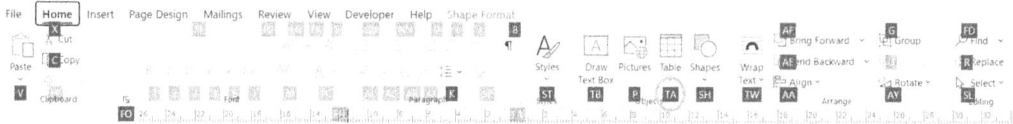

Figure 9-9 shows the available Key Tips for the Publisher Home ribbon.

Next, two **Send Keys** steps are used: the first presses the **Right Arrow** key Six times, and the second presses the **Down Arrow** key Two times to set the table dimensions. Finally, a **Keystrokes** step presses the **Enter** key to complete the process.

> When entering text in the "Send Keys" step, ensure you include a space after the code and before the value, such as in {Right 6}.

> When deciding on a command phrase that includes a number. It is best practice to write the number in word form rather than using the numeral.

Creating a Styled Table in Microsoft Publisher

This Step-by-Step command expands on the previous example. In this scenario, we create a Step-by-Step command that instructs Dragon to create a 5x4 table, format all the cells to align text to the center-right, and set the table's height to 5 cm and its width to 14 cm.

MyCommand Name: create styled five by four table

Description: Creates a styled 5 x 4 table

Group: Dragon – Microsoft Publisher Step-by-Step commands

Availability: Application-specific

Application: Microsoft Publisher

Command Type: Step-by-Step

Steps:

```
Keystrokes Press Alt + H
Send Keys Send Keys "TA"
Send Keys Send Keys "{Right 4}"
Send Keys Send Keys "{Down 3}"
Keystrokes Press Enter
Keystrokes Press Alt + J
Send Keys Send Keys "LQT"
Keystrokes Press Alt + J
Send Keys Send Keys "LCR"
Keystrokes Press Alt + J
Send Keys Send Keys "LTH"
Type Text Type "5 cm"
Keystrokes Press Tab
Type Text Type "14 cm"
Keystrokes Press Enter
```

Figure 9-10

The MyCommands Editor window, displaying the configuration for the "create styled five by four table" command and its required steps.

Ensure that MS Publisher is the active window, and try it by saying:

"create styled five by four table"

Discuss

Since this command builds on the previous one, the first five steps remain nearly identical for creating the table, with adjustments to the values used in the **Send Keys** steps.

Once the table is created, the Key Tips disappear, and as the table is the active object, Publisher activates the Table Layout ribbon. To style the table, a **Keystrokes** step emulates pressing **Alt+J**, reveals the Key Tips for the Table Layout ribbon.

Pressing the letters **L**, **Q**, and **T** in sequence selects the "Select Table" option. A single **Send Keys** step is used to emulate this sequence (Send Keys "LQT").

Next, another **Keystrokes** step (pressing **Alt+J**) reveals the Key Tips again, allowing us to use a single **Send Keys** step to press **L**, **C**, and **R** to select the "Align Center Right" option.

Figure 9-11

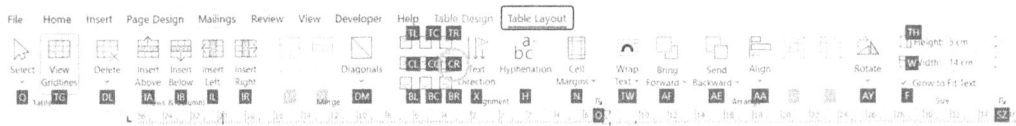

Figure 9-11 shows the available Key Tips for the Publisher Table Layout ribbon.

To adjust the table dimensions, the Height field is selected using a similar process. A **Type Text** step inputs the value **5 cm**, followed by a **Keystrokes** step pressing the **Tab** key to navigate to the Width field. Another **Type Text** step inputs the value **14 cm**. Finally, a **Keystrokes** step emulates pressing the **Enter** key to confirm the changes.

When entering text in the "Send Keys" step, ensure you include a space after the code and before the value, such as in {Right 4}.

When deciding on a command phrase that includes a number. It is best practice to write the number in word form rather than using the numeral.

Dragon Commands for MindManager

Dragon, by default, offers basic text control for the MindManager application. This is indicated by the Full Text Control Indicator (small green indicator) being turned off in the DragonBar. While some MindManager functions can be performed by dictating key presses, this approach requires memorising all the available shortcut keystrokes.

This section provides several useful Step-by-Step commands tested with **MindManager 2023 (32/64 bit)**.

While the application offers a wide range of shortcut key combinations for various functions, remembering them can be challenging. Instead, you can create Step-by-Step commands to perform popular MindManager functions by simply dictating easy-to-remember voice commands.

These commands are also compatible with earlier versions of MindManager.

In This Part: Step-by-Step Commands

66–75

Create a New MindManager Topic (List command)

Creating new topics in MindManager is a fundamental step in building mind maps. Users can create a new topic either by navigating to the MindManager **Home** ribbon and clicking the **New Topic** option or by pressing the **Enter** key on the keyboard. To perform this action by voice, we can create a **Step-by-Step List** command that allows users to dictate any of several predefined command phrases.

MyCommand Name: <mm_new_topic>

Name of List(s) used: <mm_new_topic>

List items:
new topic
add new topic
create topic
insert a new topic

Description: Creates a new MindManager topic

Group: Dragon – MindManager Step-by-Step commands

Availability: Application-specific

Application: MindManager 23

Command Type: Step-by-Step

Steps:

Keystrokes Press Enter

Figure 10-0

The MyCommands Editor window, displaying the configuration for the "<mm_new_topic>" command and its required steps.

Make sure MindManager is the active window, then try it by saying:

"add new topic"

"create topic"

"insert a new topic"

Discuss

This Step-by-Step command uses a single **Keystrokes** step to execute the MindManager shortcut by pressing **Enter** to create a new topic.

To facilitate dictation of natural language variations for creating a new topic, we have created a Dragon List command. The List named <mm_new_topic> contains all the voice command phrases that can be dictated to execute the command. You can add alternative command phrases to execute the command by editing the List.

When looking for shortcut key combinations in MindManager, most of them can be observed by positioning your mouse over the intended function.

MindManager is a part of the Windows family of applications that go a long way to providing keyboard control to access all functionalities. By pressing the Alt key, you will see several highlighted letters and numbers appear under the menus. If you know the menu that contains the function you wish to use, you can press the relative letters or numbers to navigate your way to that function. Make a note of the keys pressed to easily create a voice command to do the same.

Create a New MindManager Subtopic (List command)

Creating subtopics in MindManager is an essential part of constructing mind maps. Users can create a new subtopic either by navigating to the MindManager Home ribbon and clicking the **New Subtopic** option or by pressing the **Insert** key on the keyboard. To perform this action by voice, we can create a **Step-by-Step List** command that allows users to dictate any of several predefined command phrases.

MyCommand Name: <mm_new_subtopic>

Name of List(s) used: <mm_new_subtopic>

List items:
new subtopic
add new subtopic
create subtopic
insert a new subtopic

Description: Creates a new MindManager subtopic

Group: Dragon – MindManager Step-by-Step commands

Availability: Application-specific

Application: MindManager 23

Command Type: Step-by-Step

Steps:

Keystrokes Press Insert

Figure 10-1

The MyCommands Editor window, displaying the configuration for the "<mm_new_subtopic>" command and its required steps.

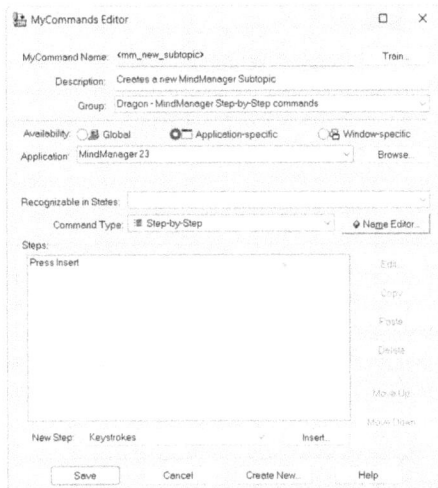

Make sure MindManager is the active window, then try it by saying:

"add new subtopic"

"create subtopic"

"insert a new subtopic"

Discuss

This Step-by-Step command uses a single **Keystrokes** step to execute the MindManager shortcut by pressing the **Insert** key to create a new subtopic.

To facilitate dictation of natural language variations for creating a new subtopic, we have created a Dragon List command. The List named `<mm_new_subtopic>` contains all the voice command phrases that can be dictated to execute the command. You can add alternative command phrases to execute the command by editing the List.

Show or Hide MindManager Topic Notes (List command)

To add, show, or hide notes for a selected topic, users can either navigate to the MindManager **Insert** ribbon and click the **Notes** option or press the **Ctrl+T** keyboard shortcut. To perform these actions by voice, a **Step-by-Step List** command can be created, enabling you to dictate any of several predefined command phrases.

MyCommand Name: <mm_show_hide_notes>

Name of List(s) used: <mm_show_hide_notes>

List items:
show notes
add notes
hide notes
hide the notes

Description: Shows or hides the selected topic's notes

Group: Dragon – MindManager Step-by-Step commands

Availability: Application-specific

Application: MindManager 23

Command Type: Step-by-Step

Steps:

Keystrokes Press Ctrl + T

Figure 10-2

The MyCommands Editor window, displaying the configuration for the "<mm_show_hide_notes>" command and its required steps.

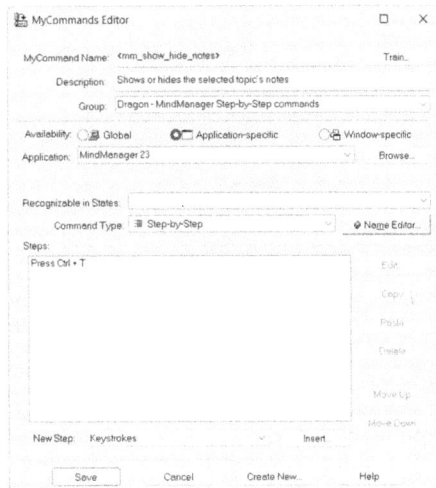

Make sure MindManager is the active window, select a topic, then try it by saying:

"show notes"
"hide notes"

Discuss

MindManager provides the keyboard shortcut **Ctrl+T** to toggle topic notes. This **Step-by-Step List** command uses a **Keystrokes** step to perform the shortcut.

To facilitate dictation of natural language variations for showing or hiding the topic notes, we have created a Dragon List command. The List named `<mm_show_hide_notes>` contains all the voice command phrases that can be dictated to execute the command. You can add alternative command phrases to execute the command by editing the List.

Adding a link to a MindManager Topic (List command)

To add a link to a topic, the **Add Link** window must be opened. This can be done by either navigating to the MindManager **Home** ribbon and clicking the **Link** option or pressing the **Ctrl+Shift+K** keyboard shortcut. To perform this action by voice, a **Step-by-Step List** command can be created, allowing you to dictate any of several predefined command phrases.

MyCommand Name: <mm_add_link>

Name of List(s) used: <mm_add_link>

List items:

add link

add link to this

add website link

open add link window

Description: Opens the Add Link window

Group: Dragon – MindManager Step-by-Step commands

Availability: Application-specific

Application: MindManager 23

Command Type: Step-by-Step

Steps:

Keystrokes Press Ctrl + Shift + K

Figure 10-3

The MyCommands Editor window, displaying the configuration for the "<mm_add_link>" command and its required steps.

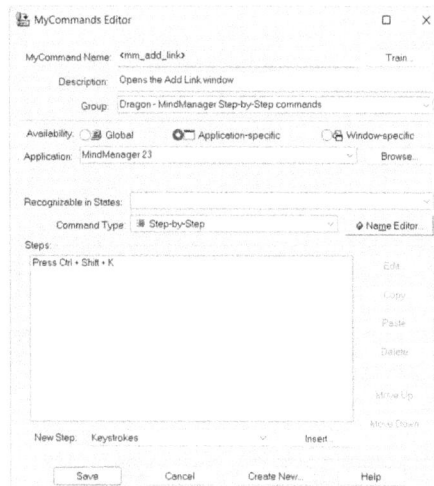

Make sure MindManager is the active window, select a topic, then try it by saying:
"add link"
"open add link window"

Discuss

MindManager provides the keyboard shortcut **Ctrl+Shift+K** to open the Add Link window. This **Step-by-Step List** command uses a **Keystrokes** step to perform the shortcut.

To facilitate dictation of natural language variations to open the **Add Link** window, we have created a Dragon List command. The List named `<mm_add_link>` contains all the voice command phrases that can be dictated to execute the command. You can add alternative command phrases to execute the command by editing the List.

Balancing the Mind Map (List command)

As mind maps grow, there is often a need to balance the map to ensure it is evenly proportioned. This can be done by either navigating to the MindManager **Design** ribbon and clicking the **Balance Map** option or pressing the **Ctrl+Alt+B** keyboard shortcut. To perform this action by voice, a **Step-by-Step List** command can be created, allowing you to dictate any of several predefined command phrases.

MyCommand Name: <mm_balance_map>

Name of List(s) used: <mm_balance_map>

List items:
balance map
balance the map

Description: Balances the map

Group: Dragon – MindManager Step-by-Step commands

Availability: Application-specific

Application: MindManager 23

Command Type: Step-by-Step

Steps:

Keystrokes Press Ctrl + Alt + B

Figure 10-4

The MyCommands Editor window, displaying the configuration for the "<mm_balance_map>" command and its required steps.

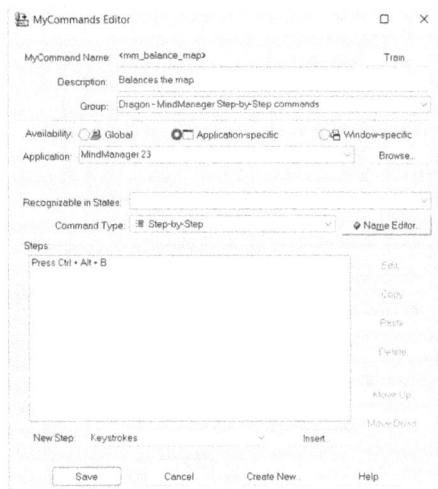

Make sure MindManager is the active window, then try it by saying:

"balance map"
"balance the map"

Discuss

MindManager provides the keyboard shortcut **Ctrl+Alt+B** to balance the map. This **Step-by-Step List** command uses a **Keystrokes** step to perform the shortcut.

To facilitate dictation of natural language variations to balance the map, we have created a Dragon List command. The List named `<mm_balance_map>` contains all the voice command phrases that can be dictated to execute the command. You can add alternative command phrases to execute the command by editing the List.

Create Five New Topics

Scenario

When planning a meeting you like to create a mind map consisting of five topics you wish to cover. To get your creative ideas flowing, you need your mind map to display five new topics. To avoid repetitive keystrokes or mouse actions, you can use a voice command that when you say, "create five topics", Dragon will perform the task for you.

This **Step-by-Step** command will carry out the task.

MyCommand Name: create five topics

Description: Creates five new topics

Group: Dragon – MindManager Step-by-Step commands

Availability: Application-specific

Application: MindManager 23

Command Type: Step-by-Step

Steps:

`Send Keys` Send Keys "{Enter 5}"

Figure 10-5

The MyCommands Editor window, displaying the configuration for the "create five topics" command and its required steps.

Make sure MindManager is the active window, select a topic, then try it by saying.
"create five topics"

Discuss

In this scenario, creating five new topics would require pressing the **Enter** key five times. Therefore, to simplify the number of steps required, we can use the **Send Keys** step by adding the value 5 to the word **Enter** within curly brackets ({Enter 5}), which will simulate pressing the **Enter** key five times.

When entering text in the "Send Keys" step, ensure you include a space after the code and before the value, such as in {Enter 5}.

When deciding on a command phrase that includes a number. It is best practice to write the number in word form rather than using the numeral.

Alternative

You can adjust the value to change the number of new topics created. For example: {Enter 3}.

Switching to the Outline View

Scenario

When creating mind maps, you may want to switch to the **Outline** view to see your work from a different perspective. To make the switch, you would typically navigate to the **View** ribbon and select the **Outline** option. This can also be achieved using a sequence of keyboard keypresses, making it possible to create a **Step-by-Step** command to perform the switch.

In this scenario, we will create a **Step-by-Step** command so that when you dictate the command phrase "switch to outline view", regardless of the ribbon you are currently viewing, Dragon performs the switch for you.

MyCommand Name: switch to outline view

Description: Switches to the Outline view

Group: Dragon – MindManager Step-by-Step commands

Availability: Application-specific

Application: MindManager 23

Command Type: Step-by-Step

Steps:

```
Keystrokes Press Alt + W
Keystrokes Press O
```

Figure 10-6

The MyCommands Editor window, displaying the configuration for the "switch to outline view" command and its required steps.

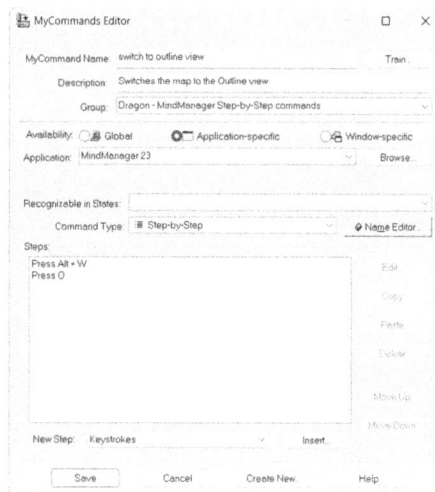

Make sure MindManager is the active window, then try it by saying:

"switch to outline view"

Discuss

In this scenario, the keyboard steps required to switch to the **Outline** view are as follows: First, use the keyboard shortcut **Alt+W** to navigate to the **View** ribbon, revealing letters under various options. Then, press the letter **O** to select the **Outline** option. Now that we know the sequence and the key presses required, we insert two **Keystrokes** steps to emulate the procedure.

Alternative

To create an alternative Step-by-Step command for switching to the **Map** view, you can make a new copy of the original command. Then, change the command phrase to something like "switch to map view" and edit the second step, replacing **Keystrokes O** with **Keystrokes M**.

Create a Topic with a Title Including the Current Date

Scenario

You are responsible for creating mind maps for staff meetings, and one of your topics always includes the title "Team Meeting Agenda:" followed by the current date.

You need a voice command that will automatically create a new topic, insert the title with a colon, and append the current date.

In this scenario, we will create a **Step-by-Step** command so that when you dictate the command phrase "create agenda topic", Dragon creates a new topic and titles it with the words "Team Meeting Agenda:" followed by the current date.

MyCommand Name: create agenda topic

Description: Creates and titles a new topic with current date

Group: Dragon – MindManager Step-by-Step commands

Availability: Application-specific

Application: MindManager 23

Command Type: Step-by-Step

Steps:

```
Keystrokes Press Enter
Type Text Type "Team Meeting Agenda: "
Keystrokes Press Alt + N
Keystrokes Press D
Keystrokes Press Enter
Wait 50 milliseconds
Keystrokes Press ESC
Keystrokes Press Enter
```

Figure 10-7

The MyCommands Editor window, displaying the configuration for the "create agenda topic" command and its required steps.

Make sure MindManager is the active window, then try it by saying:

"create agenda topic"

Discuss

This scenario involves several steps to achieve the objective. The first step creates a new topic. Next, a **Type Text** step is used to insert the required text—in this example, "Team Meeting Agenda: " is inserted. Notice that there is a space after the colon.

The remaining steps access the MindManager **Insert** menu, select the **Date & Time** option, and then simulate pressing the **Enter** key. A **Wait** step is included to ensure there is a slight delay after inserting the date. Finally, **Keystrokes** steps for **Press ESC** followed by **Press Enter** confirm the process.

> You may need to adjust the Wait time to accommodate your computer's processing speed to ensure the command works successfully.

Change Topic Shape to a Circle

Scenario

MindManager does not provide a specific keyboard shortcut to change the selected shape into a circle. However, this task can be completed either via the **Format** menu or through a sequence of keyboard keystrokes. To increase productivity and save time locating the option, we can perform this action by voice. By creating a **Step-by-Step** command, that responds to the command phrase "change shape to circle", and have Dragon perform the task for you, regardless of the ribbon you are currently viewing.

MyCommand Name: change shape to circle

Description: Changes the selected topic shape to a circle

Group: Dragon – MindManager Step-by-Step commands

Availability: Application-specific

Application: MindManager 23

Command Type: Step-by-Step

Steps:

```
Keystrokes Press Alt + M
Keystrokes Press H
Keystrokes Press Down
Send Keys Send Keys "{Right 3}"
Keystrokes Press Enter
```

Figure 10-8

The MyCommands Editor window, displaying the configuration for the "change shape to circle" command and its required steps.

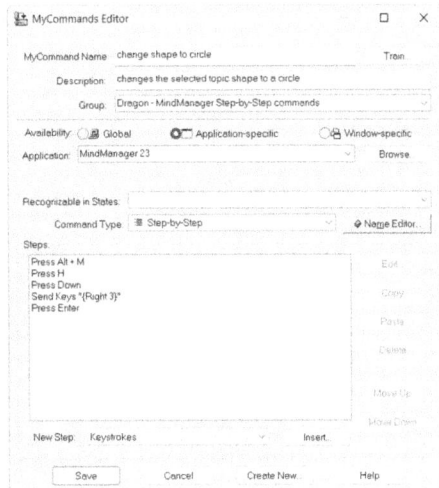

Make sure MindManager is the active window, select a topic, then try it by saying:
"change shape to circle"

Discuss

This scenario involves several steps to achieve the objective. The first two steps access the MindManager **Format** menu and select the **Topic Shape** option. The **Keystrokes** step with **Press Down** simulates pressing the **Down Arrow** key. Next, a **Send Keys** step is used to press the **Right Arrow** key three times, selecting the **Circle** option. Finally, a **Keystrokes** step with **Press Enter** applies the change.

Alternative

To create a Step-by-Step command for changing to a different shape, you will need to determine the navigation required using the arrow keys and adjust the steps accordingly.

Add the Priority One Icon to a Topic

To visually add urgency to some of your topics you can add MindManager's **Priority icons** to them.

The following **Step-by-Step** command, when executed using the command phrase "make this priority one" will add the **Priority 1** icon to the selected topic.

MyCommand Name: make this priority one

Description: Adds the Priority One icon to the selected topic

Group: Dragon – MindManager Step-by-Step commands

Availability: Application-specific

Application: MindManager 23

Command Type: Step-by-Step

Steps:

Keystrokes `Press Ctrl + Shift + 1`

Figure 10-9

The MyCommands Editor window, displaying the configuration for the "make this priority one" command and its required steps.

Make sure MindManager is the active window, select a topic, then try it by saying:
"make this priority one"

Discuss

In this scenario, we utilise the MindManager keyboard shortcut **Ctrl+Shift+1** to insert the **Priority 1** icon into the selected topic. As a result, only one **Keystrokes** step is needed.

When deciding on a command phrase that includes a number. It is best practice to write the number in word form rather than using the numeral.

Alternative

To create alternative Step-by-Step commands for inserting Priority 2–9 icons, MindManager uses the same keyboard shortcut, with the number adjusted for the desired priority. For example, **Ctrl+Shift+2** inserts the Priority 2 icon, **Ctrl+Shift+3** inserts the Priority 3 icon, and so on.

Dragon Commands for Adobe Photoshop

By default, Dragon provides basic text control for Photoshop, as indicated by the Full Text Control Indicator (a small green light) being turned off in the DragonBar. Additionally, Dragon does not include any application-specific voice commands for Photoshop. However, by leveraging Photoshop's built-in keyboard shortcuts, you can create Step-by-Step commands to perform Photoshop functions using voice commands.

Photoshop offers a wide range of shortcut key combinations for various functions, but remembering all of them can be challenging. Instead, you can create Step-by-Step commands that allow you to perform common Photoshop functions by simply dictating easy-to-remember voice commands.

This section introduces several practical Step-by-Step commands to streamline your workflow and make Photoshop more accessible through voice commands. They have been tested with Photoshop 2025 and are also compatible with earlier versions of Photoshop.

In This Part: Step-by-Step Commands

76–84

Showing or Hiding the Photoshop Rulers (List command)

This **Step-by-Step List** command enables you to toggle the visibility of Photoshop rulers. By simply dictating the voice command phrases "show the rulers" or "hide the rulers" you can effortlessly display or hide the rulers as needed.

MyCommand Name: <show_hide_ps_rulers>

Name of List(s) used: <show_hide_ps_rulers>

List items:
show the rulers
hide the rulers

Description: Shows and hides the Photoshop rulers

Group: Dragon – Adobe Photoshop Step-by-Step commands

Availability: Application-specific

Application: Adobe Photoshop 2025

Command Type: Step-by-Step

Steps:

Keystrokes Press Ctrl + R

Figure 11-0

The MyCommands Editor window, displaying the configuration for the "<show_hide_ps_rulers>" command and its required steps.

Make sure Adobe Photoshop is the active window and try it by saying:
"show the rulers", "hide the rulers"

Discuss

The Photoshop rulers can be revealed or hidden using the keyboard shortcut **Ctrl+R**, therefore, we use a **Keystrokes** step to emulate **Ctrl+R**.

As it is the same keyboard shortcut to show or hide the rulers, we create a Dragon List command to allow for natural language variations. The List, named <show_hide_ps_rulers>, contains all the voice command phrases that can trigger the command. You can edit the List to add alternative phrases for executing the command.

Opening the Canvas Size Window to Change the Canvas Size

This **Step-by-Step** command allows you to open the Canvas Size window by simply dictating the command phrase "change canvas size"

MyCommand Name: change canvas size

Description: opens the Canvas Size window

Group: Dragon – Adobe Photoshop Step-by-Step commands

Availability: Application-specific

Application: Adobe Photoshop 2025

Command Type: Step-by-Step

Steps:

Keystrokes Press Ctrl + Alt + C

Figure 11-1

The MyCommands Editor window, displaying the configuration for the "change canvas size" command and its required steps.

Make sure Adobe Photoshop is the active window and try it by saying:
"change canvas size"

Discuss

The Photoshop Canvas Size window can be opened using the keyboard shortcut **Ctrl+Alt+C**, which is emulated with a **Keystrokes** step.

Opening the Image Size Window to Change the Image Size

Whenever you need to adjust the image size, this **Step-by-Step** command allows you to open the Image Size window by dictating the command phrase "change image size"

MyCommand Name: change image size

Description: opens the Image Size window

Group: Dragon – Adobe Photoshop Step-by-Step commands

Availability: Application-specific

Application: Adobe Photoshop 2025

Command Type: Step-by-Step

Steps:

Keystrokes `Press Ctrl + Alt + I`

Figure 11-2

The MyCommands Editor window, displaying the configuration for the "change image size" command and its required steps.

Make sure Adobe Photoshop is the active window and try it by saying:
"change image size"

Discuss

The Photoshop Image Size window can be opened using the keyboard shortcut **Ctrl+Alt+I,** which is emulated with a **Keystrokes** step.

Zooming In with a Voice Command

To zoom in on your Photoshop image, simply dictate the command "Zoom In" to execute this **Step-by-Step** command.

MyCommand Name: zoom in

Description: Zooms into the image

Group: Dragon – Adobe Photoshop Step-by-Step commands

Availability: Application-specific

Application: Adobe Photoshop 2025

Command Type: Step-by-Step

Steps:

Keystrokes Press Ctrl + =

Figure 11-3

The MyCommands Editor window, displaying the configuration for the "zoom in" command and its required steps.

Make sure Adobe Photoshop is the active window and try it by saying:
"zoom in"

Discuss

The keyboard shortcut **Ctrl+=** is used to Zoom In and is emulated with a **Keystrokes** step.

Doubling the Zoom Out Effect in Photoshop

Double the default zoom-out percentage in Photoshop using this **Step-by-Step** command.

MyCommand Name: zoom out twice

Description: Zooms out twice

Group: Dragon – Adobe Photoshop Step-by-Step commands

Availability: Application-specific

Application: Adobe Photoshop 2025

Command Type: Step-by-Step

Steps:

```
Keystrokes Press Ctrl + -
Keystrokes Press Ctrl + -
```

Figure 11-4

The MyCommands Editor window, displaying the configuration for the "zoom out twice" command and its required steps.

Make sure Adobe Photoshop is the active window and try it by saying:
"zoom out twice"

Discuss

The keyboard shortcut **Ctrl+-** can be used to Zoom Out. This **Step-by-Step** command uses the **Keystrokes** step twice to perform this action.

Convert Image to Black & White

Photoshop provides a keyboard shortcut to convert an image to Black & White. Instead of trying to remember the shortcut, this Step-by-Step command allows you to convert the image to Black & White simply by dictating the command phrase "convert to black and white". This phrase is much easier to recall than the keyboard combination.

MyCommand Name: convert to black and white

Description: Converts image to Black & White

Group: Dragon – Adobe Photoshop Step-by-Step commands

Availability: Application-specific

Application: Adobe Photoshop 2025

Command Type: Step-by-Step

Steps:

```
Keystrokes Press Ctrl + Shift + Alt + B
Keystrokes Press Enter
```

Figure 11-5

The MyCommands Editor window, displaying the configuration for the "convert to black and white" command and its required steps.

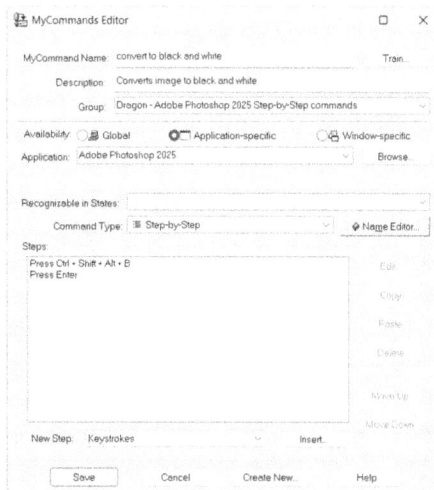

Make sure Adobe Photoshop is the active window and try it by saying:

"convert to black and white"

Discuss

Photoshop allows the use of the keyboard shortcut **Ctrl+Shift+Alt+B** to open the Black and White window. This **Step-by-Step** command uses a **Keystrokes** step to perform the shortcut, followed by another **Keystrokes** step to press the **Enter** key and complete the process.

Performing the Photoshop Trim Function

The Trim function is commonly used by Photoshop users but often requires navigating through menus, making it repetitive and time-consuming. This **Step-by-Step** command minimizes mouse and keyboard actions by enabling you to dictate the command phrase "trim transparent pixels". Dragon will then automatically open the Trim window, select Transparent Pixels, and execute the function.

MyCommand Name: trim transparent pixels

Description: Opens the Trim window and selects Transparent Pixels

Group: Dragon – Adobe Photoshop Step-by-Step commands

Availability: Application-specific

Application: Adobe Photoshop 2025

Command Type: Step-by-Step

Steps:

```
Keystrokes Press Alt + I
Send Keys Send Keys "R"
Keystrokes Press Alt + A
Keystrokes Press Enter
```

Figure 11-6

The MyCommands Editor window, displaying the configuration for the "trim transparent pixels" command and its required steps.

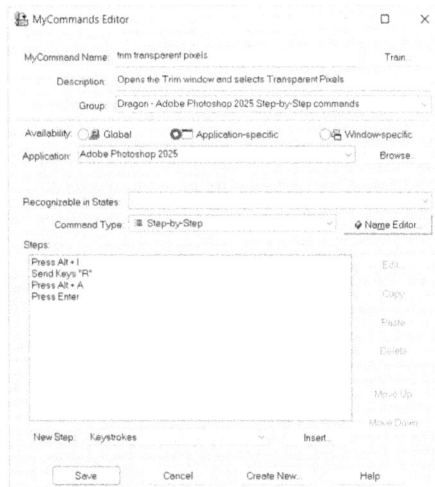

Make sure Adobe Photoshop is the active window and try it by saying:

"trim transparent pixels"

Discuss

This command consists of several steps. First, a **Keystrokes** step uses the keyboard shortcut **Ctrl+I** to reveal the Image menu. Next, a **Send Keys** step presses the letter **R** to select the Trim option and open the Trim window.

To ensure the Transparent Pixels option is selected, a **Keystrokes** step performs the keyboard shortcut **Alt+A**. Finally, a **Keystrokes** step presses the **Enter** key to complete the process.

Adobe Photoshop provides extensive keyboard control to access most functionalities. By pressing the **Alt** key, clues to the available keyboard shortcuts appear, with specific letters in options and menus underlined. For example, pressing **Alt+L** will reveal the Layer menu.

Figure 11-7

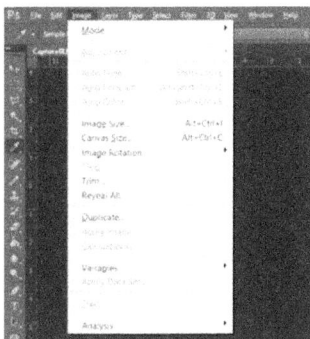

Figure 11-7 displays the Photoshop Image menu with keyboard shortcuts and underlined letters for quick access.

If you know which menu contains the function you want to use, you can press the corresponding keys to navigate to that function. Take note of the keys you press so you can easily create a voice command to perform the same action.

Applying a Motion Blur with a Specific Setting

As part of your image editing workflow, you frequently apply a specific Motion Blur effect to enhance your visuals. Manually navigating through Photoshop menus to adjust the settings can be time-consuming. You want a voice command that simplifies this process.

By dictating the command phrase "apply motion blur", Dragon will execute the Motion Blur effect, adjust the angle to 10 degrees, and set the distance to 15.

This **Step-by-Step** command streamlines the task, saving time and effort while ensuring consistency in your edits.

MyCommand Name: apply motion blur

Description: Applies Motion Blur to the image

Group: Dragon – Adobe Photoshop Step-by-Step commands

Availability: Application-specific

Application: Adobe Photoshop 2025

Command Type: Step-by-Step

Steps:

```
Keystrokes   Press Alt + T
Send Keys    Send Keys "B"
Keystrokes   Press Right
Send Keys    Send Keys "M"
Type Text    Type "25"
Keystrokes   Press Tab
Type Text    Type "115"
Keystrokes   Press Enter
```

Figure 11-8

The MyCommands Editor window, displaying the
configuration for the "apply motion blur" command and
its required steps.

Make sure Adobe Photoshop is the active window and try it by saying:

"apply motion blur"

Discuss

This command consists of several steps. First, a **Keystrokes** step uses the keyboard shortcut **Alt+T** to access the Photoshop Filter menu.

Next, a **Send Keys** step presses the letter **B** to select the Blur option, followed by a **Keystrokes** step to emulate pressing the **Right Arrow** key to expand and reveal the Blur options. A **Send Keys** step then presses the letter **M** to select the Motion option and open the Motion Blur window.

As the Angle field is selected by default, a **Type Text** step is used to insert the value **25**. A **Keystrokes** step presses the **Tab** key to navigate to the Distance field, followed by a **Type Text** step to insert the value **115**. Finally, a **Keystrokes** step presses the **Enter** key to apply the settings and complete the process.

Save For Web as a PNG-24

Often, you save your images for the web. This **Step-by-Step** command opens the Save for Web window and sets the format to PNG-24, preparing the image for saving.

MyCommand Name: save for web as PNG

Description: Opens the Save for Web window and adjusts the settings to PNG

Group: Dragon – Adobe Photoshop Step-by-Step commands

Availability: Application-specific

Application: Adobe Photoshop 2025

Command Type: Step-by-Step

Steps:

```
Keystrokes Press Ctrl + Shift + Alt + S
Keystrokes Press Tab
Send Keys Send Keys "{Down 10}"
Send Keys Send Keys "{Up 2}"
```

Figure 11-9

The MyCommands Editor window, displaying the configuration for the "save for web as PNG" command and its required steps.

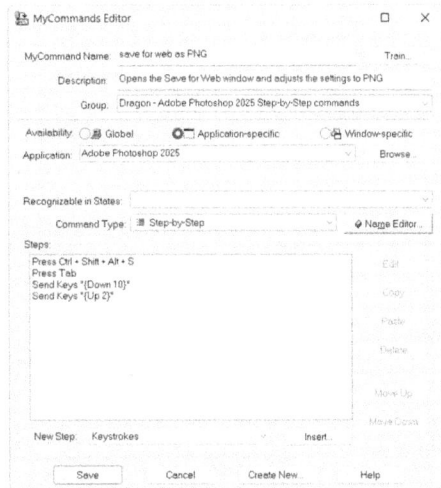

Make sure Adobe Photoshop is the active window and try it by saying:

"save for web as PNG"

Discuss

This command consists of several steps. First, a **Keystrokes** step uses the keyboard shortcut **Ctrl+Shift+Alt+S** to open the Save for Web window. Next, a **Keystrokes** step presses the **Tab** key to navigate to the Presets field.

As the Presets dropdown menu contains several options, a **Send Keys** step presses the **Down Arrow** key **10** times to ensure the bottom of the list is reached. This is followed by a **Send Keys** step pressing the **Up Arrow** key twice, as the PNG option is typically two places from the bottom of the list.

> When entering text in the "Send Keys" step, ensure you include a space after the code and before the value, such as in {Down 10}.

Dragon Commands for Sublime Text

By default, Dragon provides only basic text control for Sublime Text, as shown by the absence of the Full Text Control Indicator (a small green light) in the DragonBar. Additionally, Dragon does not offer any built-in voice commands specific to Sublime Text. However, by utilising Sublime Text's built-in keyboard shortcuts, you can create Step-by-Step commands to perform various Sublime Text functions using voice commands.

While Sublime Text includes numerous shortcut key combinations for its functions, remembering them all can be difficult. Instead, you can create Step-by-Step commands to simplify these tasks by dictating intuitive, easy-to-remember voice commands.

This section presents several practical Step-by-Step commands designed to enhance your workflow and improve accessibility in Sublime Text using voice commands. These commands have been tested with the latest version of Sublime Text, which, at the time of this book's release, is version 4.

In This Part: Step-by-Step Commands
85–94

Opening Sublime Text by Voice

By default, Dragon recognises many applications, allowing you to use voice commands like 'Open WordPad,' 'Open Paint,' 'Open Excel,' or 'Open Command Prompt' to launch them.

However, for some applications, if we wish to open them by voice, we first need to know the location of the executable file and then we can create a **Step-by-Step** command to open it.

This **Step-by-Step** command opens the Sublime Text application when you dictate the command phrase "open sublime text".

MyCommand Name: open sublime text

Description: Opens the Sublime Text application

Group: Dragon – Sublime Text Step-by-Step commands

Availability: Global

Command Type: Step-by-Step

Steps:

```
Open (application)
        Target: C:\Program Files\Sublime Text\sublime_text.exe
        Arguments:
        Start in:
        Run: Maximized
```

Figure 12-0

The MyCommands Editor window, displaying the configuration for the "open sublime text" command and its required steps.

Try it by saying:

"open sublime text"

Discuss

This command uses the **Open (application)** step to open the Sublime Text application. The breakdown is as follows: the **Target** field is populated with the full path and executable filename, including the file extension. The **Arguments** field is left blank, and the **Run** field is set to 'Maximized' so that the Sublime Text application opens in a maximized state.

The method to create this command varies depending on your version of Dragon. Specifically, in the case of Dragon Professional v16, it also depends on how Dragon was installed and whether you have administrative rights.

If the **Target** field is not available, click the Browse button to open the Choose Application or Document window. From there, navigate to the executable file of Sublime Text, select the executable, and click the Open button. The executable is typically located in: C:\Program Files\Sublime Text\sublime_text.exe.

Changing the Layout View

When working on several projects in Sublime, it is often useful to change the layout view to compare code between projects.

This **Step-by-Step** command allows you to dictate the voice command, "change layout to two columns" which utilises the keyboard shortcut provided by Sublime to switch the layout view to two columns.

MyCommand Name: change layout to two columns

Description: Changes the layout view to two columns

Group: Dragon – Sublime Text Step-by-Step commands

Availability: Application-specific

Application: Sublime Text

Command Type: Step-by-Step

Steps:

Keystrokes Press Shift + Alt + 2

Figure 12-1

The MyCommands Editor window, displaying the configuration for the "change layout to two columns" command and its required steps.

Ensure that Sublime Text is the active window and try it by saying:

"change layout to two columns"

Discuss

Changing the layout view to two columns can be achieved by using the keyboard shortcut **Shift+Alt+2**. Therefore, we use a **Keystrokes** step to emulate pressing **Shift+Alt+2**.

> When deciding on a command phrase that includes a number. It is best practice to write the number in word form rather than using the numeral.

Alternative

To create alternative **Step-by-Step** commands for changing the layout view, Sublime Text uses the same keyboard shortcut with the number adjusted for the desired layout. For example, **Shift+Alt+1** changes the view to a single layout, **Shift+Alt+3** changes the view to a three-column layout, and **Shift+Alt+4** changes the view to a four-column layout.

Swapping the Case of the Text

Sublime Text does not provide a direct keyboard shortcut to swap the case of selected text. However, this can be achieved using a sequence of keyboard presses, allowing a **Step-by-Step** command to be created for the process.

By dictating the command phrase "swap the case" this **Step-by-Step** command will execute the action seamlessly.

MyCommand Name: swap the case

Description: Swaps the case of the selected text

Group: Dragon – Sublime Text Step-by-Step commands

Availability: Application-specific

Application: Sublime Text

Command Type: Step-by-Step

Steps:

```
Keystrokes Press Alt + E
Send Keys Send Keys "A"
Send Keys Send Keys "{Down 3}"
Keystrokes Press Enter
```

Figure 12-2

The MyCommands Editor window, displaying the configuration for the "swap the case" command and its required steps.

Ensure that Sublime Text is the active window, select the text to be changed, and try it by saying:

"swap the case"

Discuss

This command begins with a **Keystrokes** step to execute the keyboard shortcut **Alt+E**, switching to the Sublime Text Edit menu and ensuring the command works regardless of the currently active menu. This shortcut also reveals the Key Tips for the Edit menu, where Sublime provides visual clues to available keyboard shortcuts, such as the line underneath the letter **A** in the Convert Case option.

Figure 12-3

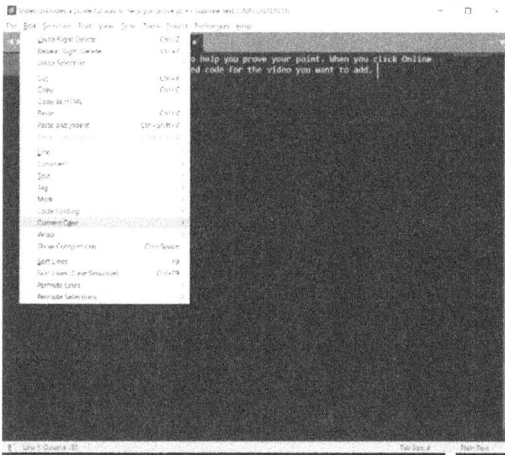

Figure 12-3 illustrates the Sublime Text application with Key Tips displayed in the Edit menu.

Next a **Send Keys** step presses the letter **A** to reveal the Convert Case options. Another **Send Keys** step presses the **Down Arrow** three times to select the Swap Case option. Finally, a **Keystrokes** step presses the **Enter** key to complete the action.

> When inserting the text within the "Send Keys" step, it is important to include a space after the code and before the value such as in {Down 3}.

Sorting the Lines of Text

To sort the lines of text, simply dictate the command "sort the lines" to execute this **Step-by-Step** command.

MyCommand Name: sort the lines

Description: Sorts the lines

Group: Dragon – Sublime Text Step-by-Step commands

Availability: Application-specific

Application: Sublime Text

Command Type: Step-by-Step

Steps:

Keystrokes Press F9

Figure 12-4

The MyCommands Editor window, displaying the configuration for the "sort the lines" command and its required steps.

Ensure that Sublime Text is the active window and try it by saying:

"sort the lines"

Discuss

By default, Sublime Text provides the **F9** keyboard shortcut to sort lines. This command uses a **Keystrokes** step to execute the shortcut.

Sort and then Permute lines Unique

Scenario

As part of your workflow, you often need to sort a list of text and then search for and remove duplicate instances. This can be immensely time-consuming, and you'd prefer a voice command that not only sorts the lines but also removes duplicates in one step.

This **Step-by-Step** command enables you to dictate the phrase "sort and permute uniquely" to have Dragon perform the task automatically.

MyCommand Name: sort and permute uniquely

Description: Sorts the list and then permute lines unique

Group: Dragon – Sublime Text Step-by-Step commands

Availability: Application-specific

Application: Sublime Text

Command Type: Step-by-Step

Steps:

```
Keystrokes Press F9
Wait Wait 50 milliseconds
Keystrokes Press Ctrl + Shift + P
Wait Wait 50 milliseconds
Type Text Type "unique"
Keystrokes Press Enter
```

Figure 12-5

The MyCommands Editor window, displaying the configuration for the "sort and permute uniquely" command and its required steps.

Ensure that Sublime Text is the active window and try it by saying:

"sort and permute uniquely"

Discuss

This command begins with a **Keystrokes** step to execute the **F9** keyboard shortcut, sorting the lines of text. A **Wait** step follows to ensure the list has been sorted before proceeding to the next **Keystrokes** step, which emulates pressing **Ctrl+Shift+P** to open the Sublime Text Command Palette. Another **Wait** step ensures the Command Palette field is ready to receive input. A **Type Text** step then inserts the word 'unique', and finally, a **Keystrokes** step presses the **Enter** key to complete the process.

You may need to adjust the Wait time to accommodate your computer's processing speed to ensure the command works successfully.

Wrapping Paragraph at 70 Characters

To wrap the paragraph at 70 characters, simply dictate the command "wrap at 70 characters" to execute this **Step-by-Step** command.

MyCommand Name: wrap at seventy characters

Description: Wraps text at 70 characters

Group: Dragon – Sublime Text Step-by-Step commands

Availability: Application-specific

Application: Sublime Text

Command Type: Step-by-Step

Steps:

```
Keystrokes Press Alt + E
Send Keys Send Keys "W"
Keystrokes Press Down
Keystrokes Press Enter
```

Figure 12-6

The MyCommands Editor window, displaying the configuration for the "wrap at seventy characters" command and its required steps.

Ensure that Sublime Text is the active window and try it by saying:

"wrap at seventy characters"

Discuss

This command starts with a **Keystrokes** step to execute the keyboard shortcut **Alt+E**, switching to the Sublime Text Edit menu and ensuring the command functions regardless of the currently active menu. A **Send Keys** step presses the letter **W** to select the Wrap option and reveal its options. Next, another **Send Keys** step presses the **Down Arrow** key, followed by a **Keystrokes** step to press **Enter** and confirm the selection.

When deciding on a command phrase that includes a number. It is best practice to write the number in word form rather than using the numeral.

Setting the Sublime Ruler at 100 Characters

Sublime Text includes a ruler feature that serves as a visual aid for managing text length. To set the ruler at 100 characters, you can simply dictate the command "set ruler at 100 characters" to execute this **Step-by-Step** command.

MyCommand Name: set ruler at one hundred characters

Description: Sets ruler at 100 characters

Group: Dragon – Sublime Text Step-by-Step commands

Availability: Application-specific

Application: Sublime Text

Command Type: Step-by-Step

Steps:

```
Keystrokes  Press Alt + V
Send Keys   Send Keys "R"
Send Keys   Send Keys "{Down 5}"
Keystrokes  Press Enter
```

Figure 12-7

The MyCommands Editor window, displaying the configuration for the "set ruler at one hundred characters" command and its required steps.

Ensure that Sublime Text is the active window and try it by saying:

"set ruler at one hundred characters"

Discuss

This command starts with a **Keystrokes** step to execute the keyboard shortcut **Alt+V**, switching to the Sublime Text View menu and ensuring the command functions regardless of the currently active menu. A **Send Keys** step presses the letter **R** to select the Ruler option and display its choices. Next, another **Send Keys** step presses the **Down Arrow** key **five** times, followed by a **Keystrokes** step to press **Enter** and confirm the selection.

When deciding on a command phrase that includes a number. It is best practice to write the number in word form rather than using the numeral.

When inserting the text within the "Send Keys" step, it is important to include a space after the code and before the value such as in {Down 5}.

Wrapping Paragraph Text at the Ruler

This convenient **Step-by-Step** command allows you to quickly set the paragraph wrap at the ruler. Simply dictate the command phrase "wrap at the ruler" to execute the action.

MyCommand Name: wrap at the ruler

Description: Wraps text at ruler

Group: Dragon – Sublime Text Step-by-Step commands

Availability: Application-specific

Application: Sublime Text

Command Type: Step-by-Step

Steps:

Keystrokes Press Alt + Q

Figure 12-8

The MyCommands Editor window, displaying the configuration for the "wrap at the ruler" command and its required steps.

Ensure that Sublime Text is the active window and try it by saying:

"wrap at the ruler"

Discuss

By default, Sublime Text provides the **Alt+Q** keyboard shortcut to Wrap Paragraph at Ruler. This command uses a **Keystrokes** step to execute the shortcut.

Toggling the Regular Expressions function (List command)

By default, Dragon does not include specific voice commands to toggle the regular expressions function in Sublime Text. However, since this task can be performed using a keyboard shortcut, you can create a **Step-by-Step List** command to execute the action by voice.

This **Step-by-Step List** command enables you to use the voice command phrases "turn on regular expressions" or "turn off regular expressions" to toggle the function on or off effortlessly.

MyCommand Name: <toggle_regular_expressions>

Name of List(s) used: <toggle_regular_expressions>

List items:
turn on regular expressions
turn off regular expressions

Description: Toggles the Regular Expressions function

Group: Dragon – Sublime Text Step-by-Step commands

Availability: Application-specific

Application: Sublime Text

Command Type: Step-by-Step

Steps:

Keystrokes Press Alt + R

Figure 12-9

The MyCommands Editor window, displaying the configuration for the "<toggle_regular_expressions>" command and its required steps.

Ensure that Sublime Text is the active window and try it by saying:

"turn on regular expressions"

"turn off regular expressions"

Discuss

Toggling the regular expression function can be achieved by using the keyboard shortcut **Alt+R**. Therefore, we use a **Keystrokes** step to emulate pressing **Alt+R**.

As it is the same keyboard shortcut to turn the function on or off, we create a Dragon List command to allow for natural language variations. The List, named `<toggle_regular_expressions>`, contains all the voice command phrases that can trigger the command. You can edit the List to add alternative phrases for executing the command.

Automating Text Extraction with Regular Expressions

Do you often work with regular expressions? If so, you know how easy it is to make mistakes or struggle to remember the exact syntax required for your task.

Recalling the intricacies of the regular expressions language can be challenging.

This **Step-by-Step** command inserts regular expression code into Sublime Text to automatically remove all text after a colon, leaving only the text before it.

Figure 12-10

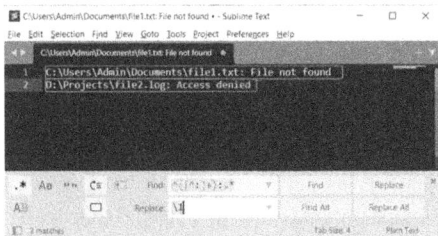

Figure 12-10 shows the Sublime Text application with the Find & Replace section on show, populated with a regular expression.

MyCommand Name: remove text after colon

Description: Runs Regular Expression to removes the text after colon

Group: Dragon – Sublime Text Step-by-Step commands

Availability: Application-specific

Application: Sublime Text

Command Type: Step-by-Step

Steps:

```
Keystrokes Press Ctrl + H
Wait Wait 50 milliseconds
Keystrokes Press Ctrl + A
Type Text Type "^([^:]+):.*"
Keystrokes Press Tab
Keystrokes Press Ctrl + A
Type Text Type "\1"
Wait Wait 50 milliseconds
Keystrokes Press Ctrl + Alt + Enter
```

Figure 12-11

The MyCommands Editor window, displaying the configuration for the "remove text after colon" command and its required steps.

Ensure that Sublime Text is the active window, the Regular Expression option is switched on, and then try it by saying:

"remove text after colon"

Discuss

This command begins with a **Keystrokes** step to execute the **Ctrl+H** keyboard shortcut, opening the Find and Replace dialog box. A **Wait** step ensures the dialog box is displayed before the next **Keystrokes** step, which presses **Ctrl+A** to select any text in the Find field.

A **Type Text** step then inserts the regular expression (^([^:]+):.*). A **Keystrokes** step presses the **Tab** key to navigate to the Replace field, followed by another **Keystrokes** step to press **Ctrl+A** and select any existing text in the field. A **Type Text** step inserts the regular expression (\1). After a **Wait** step, a final **Keystrokes** step executes the **Ctrl+Alt+Enter** shortcut to perform the Replace All function.

This command requires the Regular Expression option to be enabled.

You may need to adjust the Wait time to accommodate your computer's processing speed to ensure the command works successfully.

Dragon Commands for Mozilla Thunderbird

By default, Dragon provides only basic text control for Mozilla Thunderbird (Thunderbird), as shown by the absence of the Full Text Control Indicator (a small green light) in the DragonBar. Additionally, Dragon does not offer any built-in voice commands specific to Thunderbird. However, by utilising Thunderbird's built-in keyboard shortcuts, you can create Step-by-Step commands to perform various Thunderbird functions using voice commands.

Thunderbird provides many shortcut key combinations for its functions, but they can be hard to memorise. Alternatively, you can create Step-by-Step commands to streamline these tasks using straightforward and easy-to-remember voice commands.

This section presents several practical Step-by-Step commands designed to enhance your workflow and improve accessibility in Mozilla Thunderbird using voice commands. These commands have been tested with the latest version of Mozilla Thunderbird, which, at the time of this book's release, is version 115.18.0.

In This Part: Step-by-Step Commands
95–101

Creating a New Email in Mozilla Thunderbird (List command)

Creating a new email in Mozilla Thunderbird is probably one of the most common tasks. You can do this by navigating to the File menu, selecting New, and then choosing Message, by clicking the New Message button, or by using the keyboard shortcut Ctrl+N.

To perform this action using voice commands, you can create a **Step-by-Step List** command that enables you to dictate one of several predefined command phrases.

MyCommand Name: <mt_new_email>

Name of List(s) used: <mt_new_email>

List items:

create new email

compose email

create new message

Description: Creates a new Mozilla Thunderbird email

Group: Dragon – Mozilla Thunderbird Step-by-Step commands

Availability: Application-specific

Application: Thunderbird

Command Type: Step-by-Step

Steps:

Keystrokes Press Ctrl + N

Figure 13-0

The MyCommands Editor window, displaying the
configuration for the "<mt_new_email>" command
and its required steps.

Make sure Mozilla Thunderbird is the active window, then try it by saying:

"create new email"

"compose email"

"create new message"

Discuss

This Step-by-Step command uses a single **Keystrokes** step to execute the Mozilla Thunderbird shortcut by pressing **Ctrl+N** to create a new email.

To facilitate dictation of natural language variations for creating a new email, we have created a Dragon List command. The List named <mt_new_email> contains all the voice command phrases that can be dictated to execute the command. You can add alternative command phrases to execute the command by editing the List.

Write an Email to a Specific Person and BCC Yourself in

Scenario

As part of your job, you frequently write emails to a specific person and BCC yourself in. You want a voice command that, when used within Mozilla Thunderbird, opens a new email, automatically populates the To: field with the person's email address, inserts your email address into the Bcc field, and places the cursor in the Subject field, ready for you to dictate the subject text.

This voice command replaces the individual steps required to carry out such a task when Jane Smith is the intended recipient.

MyCommand Name: email jane smith

Description: Creates a new email to Jane Smith and BCC me in

Group: Dragon – Mozilla Thunderbird Step-by-Step commands

Availability: Application-specific

Application: Thunderbird

Command Type: Step-by-Step

Steps:

```
Keystrokes Press Ctrl + N
Type Text Type "jane.smith@theiremail.com"
Keystrokes Press Ctrl + Shift + B
Type Text Type "myemail@youremail.com"
Keystrokes Press Tab
Keystrokes Press Tab
```

Figure 13-1

The MyCommands Editor window, displaying the configuration for the "email jane smith" command and its required steps.

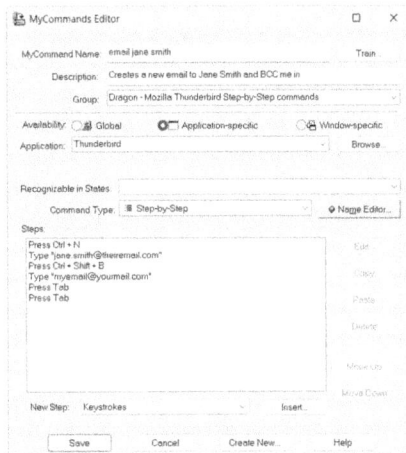

Make sure Mozilla Thunderbird is the active window and try it by saying:

"email jane smith"

Discuss

This command consists of several steps to automate the process of composing a new email with an intended recipient in Mozilla Thunderbird. First, a **Keystrokes** step uses the keyboard shortcut **Ctrl+N1** to create a new email and automatically place the cursor in the **To:** field. Next, a **Type Text** step is used to enter the desired email address.

Another **Keystrokes** step is used to perform the keyboard shortcut **Ctrl+Shift+B** which reveals the BCC field and places the cursor within it. Another **Type Text** step is used, this time to insert your own email address.

Finally, a two **Keystrokes** steps presses the **Tab** key twice to navigate to the Subject field, ready for you to dictate the email subject.

Alternative

You can create your own version by creating a new copy of the command, editing the command phrase required to execute the command in the **MyCommand Name** field, and edit the recipient's email address by updating the email address entered in the **Type Text** step.

Additionally, if you want to move the cursor directly to the body of the email, you can add another **Keystrokes** step to press **Tab** at the end. This allows you to start typing the content of your email immediately, without needing to manually click in the body area.

Reply to Only the Sender of a Message

Mozilla Thunderbird provides a keyboard shortcut to reply to the sender of a message.

This **Step-by-Step** command takes advantage of the keyboard shortcut to open the email in a new window, ready for you to reply when you dictate the phrase "reply to sender".

MyCommand Name: reply to sender

Description: Replies to the sender of a message

Group: Dragon – Mozilla Thunderbird Step-by-Step commands

Availability: Application-specific

Application: Thunderbird

Command Type: Step-by-Step

Steps:

```
Keystrokes Press Ctrl + R
```

Figure 13-2

The MyCommands Editor window, displaying the configuration for the "reply to sender" command and its required steps.

Make sure Mozilla Thunderbird is the active window, select a message, and try it by saying:
"reply to sender"

Discuss

Mozilla Thunderbird provides the **Ctrl+R** keyboard shortcut to reply to sender. This command uses a **Keystrokes** step to execute the shortcut.

Alternative

You can create your own version of this command to reply to all by duplicating the existing command, updating the command phrase in the MyCommand Name field, and modifying the **Keystrokes** step to replace `"Press Ctrl + R"` with `"Press Ctrl + Shift + R"`.

Zooming In on the Message Text

To zoom in on your Mozilla Thunderbird email text, simply dictate the command "Zoom In" to execute this **Step-by-Step** command.

MyCommand Name: zoom in

Description: Zooms in to the message text

Group: Dragon – Mozilla Thunderbird Step-by-Step commands

Availability: Application-specific

Application: Thunderbird

Command Type: Step-by-Step

Steps:

Keystrokes Press Ctrl + =

Figure 13-3

The MyCommands Editor window, displaying the configuration for the "zoom in" command and its required steps.

Make sure Mozilla Thunderbird is the active window, select a message, and try it by saying: *"zoom in"*

Discuss

The keyboard shortcut **Ctrl+=** is used to Zoom In and is emulated with a **Keystrokes** step.

Tagging Your Messages (List command)

Applying tags to your emails is a great way to categorize and easily identify specific messages within your inbox. This practice allows you to quickly locate relevant emails by searching for their associated tags, especially when managing a large volume of correspondence.

This **Step-by-Step List** command applies the first tag to the selected email when you dictate either the command phrase "apply tag one" or "tag as important".

MyCommand Name: <mt_tagging>

Name of List(s) used: <mt_tagging>

List items:

apply tag one

tag as important

Description: Applies a Tag to the selected message

Group: Dragon – Mozilla Thunderbird Step-by-Step commands

Availability: Application-specific

Application: Thunderbird

Command Type: Step-by-Step

Steps:

Send Keys Send Keys "1"

Figure 13-4

The MyCommands Editor window, displaying the configuration for the "<mt_tagging>" command and its required steps.

Make sure Mozilla Thunderbird is the active window, select a message, and then try it by saying:

"apply tag one"

"tag as important"

Discuss

This **Step-by-Step** command uses a single **Send Keys** step to press the letter **1** to apply Tag number one to the selected message.

To facilitate dictation of natural language variations for applying a Tag to the selected message, we have created a Dragon List command. The List named <mt_tagging> contains all the voice command phrases that can be dictated to execute the command. You can add alternative command phrases to execute the command by editing the List.

> When deciding on a command phrase that includes a number. It is best practice to write the number in word form rather than using the numeral.

Switching to Day View in the Thunderbird Calendar

This **Step-by-Step** command switches the calendar view to "Day" when you dictate the command phrase "switch to day view".

MyCommand Name: switch to day view

Description: Switches to the day view

Group: Dragon – Mozilla Thunderbird Step-by-Step commands

Availability: Application-specific

Application: Thunderbird

Command Type: Step-by-Step

Steps:

```
Keystrokes Press Alt + 3
Keystrokes Press Alt + V
Send Keys Send Keys "N"
Send Keys Send Keys "D"
```

Figure 13-5

The MyCommands Editor window, displaying the configuration for the "switch to day view" command and its required steps.

Make sure Mozilla Thunderbird is the active window, and try it by saying:

"switch to day view"

Discuss

This command begins with a **Keystrokes** step to execute the keyboard shortcut **Alt+3**, to switch to the Thunderbird Calendar and ensuring the command works regardless of the currently active view. Another **Keystrokes** step (Press Alt + V) is used to reveal the View menu where Thunderbird provides visual clues to available keyboard shortcuts, such as the line underneath the letter **N** in the Calendar option.

A **Send Keys** step is then used to press the letter **N** to reveal the Calendar options, followed by another **Send Keys** step to press the letter **D** to select the Day view.

Marking the Selected Read Message As Unread

This **Step-by-Step** command enables you to mark the selected read message as Unread by simply dictating the voice command phrase "mark as unread".

MyCommand Name: mark as unread

Description: Marks the selected message as Unread

Group: Dragon – Mozilla Thunderbird Step-by-Step commands

Availability: Application-specific

Application: Thunderbird

Command Type: Step-by-Step

Steps:

```
Keystrokes Press Alt + M
Send Keys Send Keys "K"
Send Keys Send Keys "U"
```

Figure 13-6

The MyCommands Editor window, displaying the configuration for the "mark as unread" command and its required steps.

Make sure Mozilla Thunderbird is the active window, select a read message, and try it by saying:
"mark as unread"

Discuss

This command begins with a **Keystrokes** step to press the keyboard shortcut **Alt+M**, revealing the Message menu. Next, two **Send Keys** steps are used: the first presses the letter **K** to select the Mark option, and the second presses the letter **U** to mark the selected message as Unread.

Section 14: Appendix

Send Keys Step Code Reference Table

Table A-1 lists the codes that the Send Keys Step supports when creating Step-by-Step commands.

Table A-1

Key	Code
ADD	{ADD}
APPLICATIONS	{APPLICATIONS} or {APPS}
BACKSPACE	{BACKSPACE} or {BS}
BREAK	{BREAK}
CANCEL	{CANCEL}
CAPS LOCK	{CAPSLOCK}
CLEAR	{CLEAR}
DECIMAL	{DECIMAL}
DELETE or DEL	{DELETE} or {DEL}
DIVIDE	{DIVIDE}
DOWN ARROW	{DOWN}
END	{END}
ENTER	{ENTER}
ESC	{ESCAPE} or {ESC}
EXECUTE	{EXECUTE} or {EXEC}
F1-F24	{F1} through {F24}
HELP	{HELP}
HOME	{HOME}
INSERT	{INSERT}
LBUTTON	{LBUTTON} or {LBTN}

Key	Code
LEFT ARROW	{LEFT}
MBUTTON	{MBUTTON} or {MBTN}
MULTIPLY	{MULTIPLY}
NUMPAD0	{NUMPAD0} or {NP0}
NUMPAD1	{NUMPAD1} or {NP1}
NUMPAD2	{NUMPAD2} or {NP2}
NUMPAD3	{NUMPAD3} or {NP3}
NUMPAD4	{NUMPAD4} or {NP4}
NUMPAD5	{NUMPAD5} or {NP5}
NUMPAD6	{NUMPAD6} or {NP6}
NUMPAD7	{NUMPAD7} or {NP7}
NUMPAD8	{NUMPAD8} or {NP8}
NUMPAD9	{NUMPAD9} or {NP9}
PAGE DOWN	{PGDN}
PAGE UP	{PGUP}
PRINT	{PRINT}
RBUTTON	{RBUTTON} or {RBTN}
RETURN	{RETURN}
RIGHT ARROW	{RIGHT}
SCROLL LOCK	{SCROLLLOCK}
SELECT	{SELECT}
SEPARATOR	{SEPARATOR}
SNAPSHOT	{SNAPSHOT}
SPACE	{SPACE}
SUBTRACT	{SUBTRACT}
TAB	{TAB}

Key	Code
UP ARROW	{UP}
WINDOWS	{WINDOWS} or {WIN}

CTRL	^
SHIFT	+
ALT	%

Including Modifier Keys

Key sequences including modifier keys can be executed using the symbols ^ (CTRL), + (SHIFT), or % (ALT). For example, to perform the key combination **CTRL+Right Arrow**, use ^{RIGHT}. Notice that the ^ sign is placed outside the brackets.

Repeating Key Sequences

Key sequences can be repeated by adding a number inside the brackets. For example, to press the **Enter** key three times, use {ENTER 3}. Make sure there is a space between the key name and the number.

Index

DRAGON PROFESSIONAL
LEARNING HUB
Reinforce Your Learning & Discover More

Unlock the Full Potential of Dragon Professional Software!

Access over 140 video tutorials (11+ hours). Refresh your Dragon expertise or enhance it further.

For Beginners to Advanced users

Includes tutorials on:
- Best practices for dictation
- Dragon's built-in commands
- Using Dragon with popular applications
- Creating your own bespoke Dragon commands
- And so much more...

Enjoy moderated community membership, quizzes, and exclusive resources designed to boost your productivity using Dragon.

Find out more at:
www.dragonspeechacademy.com

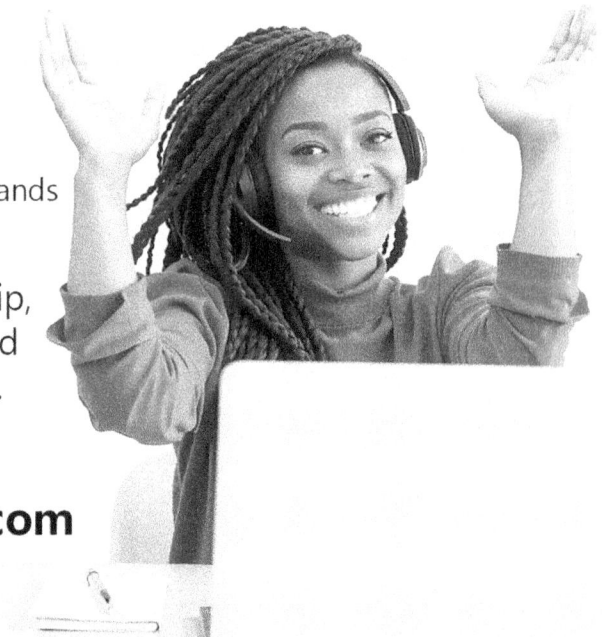

www.ingramcontent.com/pod-product-compliance
Lightning Source LLC
Chambersburg PA
CBHW081806200326
41597CB00023B/4171